AQUAPONICS BUSINESS

A Complete Walkthrough of Building Your Own
System With Step by Step Directions

(The Beginner's Guide to Harvest Fresh
Vegetables)

John Glover

D1225429

Published by Kevin Dennis

John Glover

All Rights Reserved

Aquaponics Business: A Complete Walkthrough of Building Your Own System With Step by Step Directions (The Beginner's Guide to Harvest Fresh Vegetables)

ISBN 978-1-989965-43-6

Legal & Disclaimer

The information contained in this book is not designed to replace or take the place of any form of medicine or professional medical advice. The information in this book has been provided for educational and entertainment purposes only.

The information contained in this book has been compiled from sources deemed reliable, and it is accurate to the best of the Author's knowledge; however, the Author cannot guarantee its accuracy and validity and cannot be held liable for any errors or omissions. Changes are periodically made to this book. You must consult your doctor or get professional medical advice before using any of the suggested remedies, techniques, or information in this book.

Table of Contents

Introduction

This "Aquaponics" book contains proven steps and strategies on how to plan, set up and maintain an aquaponics system right in your own home or backyard. The system may look a bit intimidating, but this book will walk you through every step.

In this book, you will learn the following:

What aquaponics is all about

What types of systems can be used

What are the basic units

What are the benefits

How to set up your own system

How to choose fishes and plants

Success tips

And so much more.

Read this book and learn everything there is to know about aquaponics.

Thanks again for purchasing this book, I hope you enjoy it!

Chapter 1: What Is Aquaponics?

Aquaponics is essentially a system in which fish and plants work together so that both can thrive. The two are cultivated together by way of a system built that utilizes recirculation of its natural biological processes. This ecological system involves waste production from the fish to be processed by bacteria and repurposed into necessary plant food that will then clean the water for the fish. Each plays a helping hand in the Aquaponics system that allows people to have an abundance of environmentally friendly, healthy, fresh food sources of both vegetation and fish. This system was born from the combination of the best parts of Hydroponics and Aquaculture, while removing the negatives associated with both, such as chemical additives for fertilization, the need for discarding water, and filtration.

HISTORY AND CURRENT USES

Aquaponics may be on the rise in familiarity and use amongst both commercial farmers and home growers, but it is certainly not a new concept. We simply get the privilege of using the new and improved, and much easier versions of Aquaponics. As they say, history repeats itself, and those that are wise will learn from those before us. It will never cease to amaze me how centuries ago, before technology, before machinery, before mass communication and social networks, our ancestors were able to create such great inventions that allowed their people to not just survive but thrive, in many areas where the environment seemed to be a major impediment.

In some form or another, Aquaponics was used throughout the continent in places like China's rice paddy fields, in Africa, in Italy, throughout the islands, by Native Americans, and the Aztecs in Mexico, to name a few. The Aztecs migrated to an area that is known today as Mexico City.

The land there did not have good soil for farming and the inner areas were all marshes. In order to adapt to this unproductive environment, they created numerous rafts on the lake out of substances found in the area, such as reeds and mud. On the rafts, they made gardens that utilized the nutrients from the aquatic species in the water to feed the plants.

Back in the day when people lived off the land, (in some places, they still do), it was vital to observe nature, take its natural processes, and use it in all aspects of life. Because of these observations, we have Aquaponics today! It is also important to note that in third world countries - just like the Aztecs so many centuries ago - faced obstacles in their environment such as bad soil, lack of water, and many people were starving. Many organizations are stepping in and introducing Aquaponics due to their fast-food growth without much water and soil-free gardening capabilities. In addition to a much-needed food source, it offers healthier, cleaner eating with much-needed vitamins and nutrients to aid in improving immune systems and fighting illness. The added bonus: Helping to prevent disease in one part of the world, stops the spread of disease to other parts of the world!

Chapter 2: Creative Growing With Aquaponics

If you're looking to find new ways of growing with aquaponics, then you're probably faced with a problem. While this type of gardening has its own challenges, sometimes we are faced with ones we just can't avoid. The biggest problem that most aquaponics enthusiasts face is space. You'll need enough space to deal with the tank, the grow beds (if you're using them), equipment, storage, access to water and power, and enough light for plants to grow. It's not an easy balance to achieve in the first place but when faced with an environment that isn't conducive to growing plants successfully sometimes you have to get creative.

Space

If your first obstacle is space, then you're going to need to look at growing upwards. This means creating vertical towers or guttering arrangements that are held above your fish tank. Your fish won't be affected by lower light, and it will help you keep the algae bloom down by shading the tank. Your compromise with such a system is that you're going to be limited on the type of plants you can grow. Plants that have large root systems or that require extra stabilization will not work in smaller containers. While this might seem like common sense, you can also look at different varieties as a way around the problem. For example, if you want to grow tomato plants but just can't give up the space for a large grow bed, compromise with a hanging variety that can be grown in guttering instead.

You can also maximize your space by growing your plants strategically. Grow large plants at the back or center of the grow box and grow smaller plants between the others or in front. This will give you the option of growing more plants per box than trying to grow all the same crops at the same time in each. As long as your system is flooding high enough to saturate the grow bed enough to reach all the plants, your only limit is how they are organized and whether you have enough fish to support them.

Light

If you're growing inside or trying to fit a lot of plants together, then lighting can be a problem. To get around this, consider using reflective panels indoors to maximize your light. Reflectors work to bounce any light rays that aren't aimed at your plants back at them. They also reflect heat, so if you're working with a system that needs heating (for example, in winter), then you won't be paying as much for heating by using reflectors. Reflectors can work outside, but because the sun's rays are so strong, they are not advised. A strong reflection can burn plants, melt plastic, and set fire to items, all of which can happen with sun rays when compared to weaker artificial light.

Water/Nutrients

There really isn't a compromise when it comes to the size of your pump. If there's one thing you should opt to go bigger with, it is the pump. The pump is what pushes water and nutrients around your system, and if it's not strong enough you'll find that the plants that are further from the water input may not get watered at all, or in a grow bed environment the water level may not reach the roots. Plants must have water and nutrients, or they will die, there is no compromise. What you can get creative with here is to have two smaller pumps as your system grows and create two smaller systems cycling off a large fish tank. This will also be a cost effective way of growing your system without wasting the pump equipment you already have.

Because your fish provide the nutrition, you also can't compromise on the size of your tank. Without enough fish, plants will not get the nutrients they need to thrive. Too many fish, and the overcrowding can cause disease, death, and fights depending on your variety. You can, however, compromise on your type of fish. Some fish are much larger than others and simply opting for a smaller variety can mean you'll be able to get more fish per tank. This will up your nutrient level in the water. The same can be said for choosing certain varieties of fish over others since they produce greater amounts of waste.

Heat

While most plants will not need extra heating in an indoor environment if you want to grow year-round you'll have to consider heating. Tropical fish species like Tilapia also require heating if you plan on growing year round in a non-tropical climate. To maximize your heat, insulate the fish tank well and consider adding a reflective cover in summer and a black one in winter if you're growing outside. Black absorbs heat while the reflective surface will direct it away on hot days. You can also help maximize your heat by using reflective panels on your lighting if you're indoors. The problem with this is that it's easy to overheat your plants and your fish so you'll also need a ventilation system.

So, the first thing to do when figuring out the best way to grow is to look at what problems you're facing with your space and tackle them accordingly. Let's see a few of the alternative ways you can set up a system to grow plants well.

Chapter 3: What Is Aquaponics And How Does It Work?

In order to understand what Aquaponics are, it is important to understand why we call it "Aquaponics." This name comes from the combination between "aquaculture" and "hydroponics". Aquaculture is the rearing, cultivating, and harvesting of different animals and plants that live in a water environment. Hydroponic refers to growing plants in an environment without soil, such as in water, sand, or gravel, and adding nutrients to those various substances. Aquaponics was created as a way for plants to grow using water around the roots and aqua animals in the water the plant is growing in; the excrement from the aqua life is broken down into nutrients for the plant. The plant does not produce food for the fish, so you will need to continue their feeding schedule.

The availability of high-quality fish has been decreasing over the last several decades. Overfishing, habitat destruction, and ecological damage has decreased the overall number of fish available for American consumption. As a result, fish farms started springing up as a way to manage the decrease in fish population. These fish farms became experts in aquaculture, the rearing, and cultivating, of aqua-life, primarily fish.

Soon, fish farms became the fastest growing food industry in the world. Aquaculture farming is much like farming that is used for chicken and beef; large water systems and pools are full of water and fish. Fish farms are also used for bait, growing algae, and supplying fish and plants for pet stores and aquariums. It can also be used to increase a population of a fish that has become endangered, or threatened by extinction.

The different forms of aquaculture include fish farms, mariculture, algaculture, and integrated multitrophic aquaculture; each one of these systems produces different products and provides different uses. Mariculture is the cultivation of animals or plants that require a saltwater environment. Examples of these types of products include many types of shell fish, finfish, like flounder, and sea plants, like seaweed. This type of system is either set up in the ocean, where the environment is already perfect for the organisms, with large nets or tanks put in the ocean water, or in tanks outside the ocean filled with salt water.

Fish farms are the most common form of aquaculture, the purpose of this system is to create fish for human consumption. About half the world's fish consumption comes from fish farms; this industry has tripled in the last twenty years. The most common fish produced in fish farms are salmon, catfish, trout, cod, and tilapia. There have been several recent legislative acts created for the purpose of regulating the booming industry.

Algaculture is the cultivation of algae, such as phytoplankton and seaweed. These types of products are created for fish food, feed for other animals, nutritional supplements, for human consumption. This particular type of system is very difficult to oversee, primarily the small algae, which is susceptible to small changes in environment. Algae requires very specific lighting, temperature, and nutrition. There are two types of systems used to cultivate algae, open-pond systems and closed-pond systems. Open pong systems are primarily used because they are generally easy to construct, less expensive, and typically produce the most amount of product. However, controlling for light and temperature is difficult. Closed-pond systems are similar to open pond systems, but they are covered controlling for both light and temperature. This type of system produces less product because it is usually smaller and more difficult to build. There are variations of different closed and open-pond systems, however we won't cover this topic as in depth as that.

Lastly, the integrated multitrophic aquaculture system is a more advanced system incorporating many different types of species into one system. The excrement from one species can be used as fertilizer for another species, for example shellfish get their nutrients from shrimp and fish droppings. It is important to understand the basic components and how they work in an aquaculture, or for our purposes, an aquaponic system, prior to starting a complex environment like this system. The purpose behind this system is balance; you are creating a symbiotic relationship where both species benefit from each other's presence.

As mentioned above, understanding the components of the Aquaponics system will help you better understand how the system works. So now that you understand a little about aquaculture, allow me to give you a brief overview of hydroponics. As mentioned before, hydroponics is a system of growing plants without soil, in sand, gravel, and water. There are several different systems within each system, however the largest difference between these systems is the medium used to house the plants.

Plants suspended in water without a growing medium is called "nutrient film technique". This technique was discovered by Dr. Alan Cooper in the 1960's at the Glasshouse Crops Research Institute in the U.K. This technique is comprised of plants suspended in plastic material, the plant roots fall into shallow water with a flowing water system flowing to each plant. Nutrients are added to the water that are then dispersed to each plant in the system. This is very popular because of its simple design and inexpensive set up. Small, and generally fast growing, plants are best for this kind of system.

Do not let these "simple" systems fool you; although they are more simple to set up, this does not mean they are necessarily "easy". However, there are many websites that tell you how to build these systems and how to set up water flow, as well as kits that include all the materials you need to start your own. Less nutrients are used for this system because of the flow of water within the system and the recirculation of the water; this system also allows for effortless temperature control. Additionally, these systems do best in a greenhouse environment, getting a lot of sun, or an inside room with artificial light.

From these two systems, Aquaponics was born. This system was first used hundreds of thousands of years ago. There is debate as to when the system was actually first used, however evidence suggests it was used in ancient Mexico where Aztecs used to grow plants on top of rafts in a pond or lake. These rafts comprised a series of "islands" known as "chinampas", which were a series of canals and rafts using mud enriched with nutrients and canals for water flow.

This was also a popular practice for cultures in the East, where fish was a major part of their diet. Even 2,000 years ago, fishmongers in China would sell live fish in baskets and bamboo cages. The rice paddy systems in Asia were also comprised of aquaponic elements; rice paddies floated on the surface of the lake or pond, and fish swam beneath the surface that provided nutrients. In a more advanced aquaponic system, multiple species were used to create a symbiotic relationship. Ducks were housed in cages over the fish ponds, the fish processed the duck droppings in the first pond, the fish in the lower pond lived on the waste that flowed from the first pond, which then flowed into a field with rice and vegetable crops. The water would flow from the first pond down to the crops already fertilized and full of nutrients.

As exploration and trade in grew, so did this practice. Fish farming caught on faster and soon the fish trade became very popular, which led to one of the first times in history that people experienced over fishing consequences. Where modern France currently is, the cultivation of oysters was common, as well as the production of fish for consumption in Rome.

Eventually as trade and transportation became easier, the need for European aquaculture decreased.

The term "Aquaponics" was coined in the 1970s. This practice became necessary because fish farmers were trying to figure out how to continue farming fish while not having to depend on land and water resources. A fisherman's livelihood depended on the amount of fish he could sell. As a result, a system called Recirculating Aquaculture Systems (RAS) was created. This system allowed large amount of fish in a small space. It produced higher yields while also producing a large amount of waste.

Beginning in the 1970s research began to study the use of plants to filter fish waste. Dr. James Rakocy, at the University of the Virgin Islands, was the main researcher identifying how plants could be used in an aquaculture system. The 1980's marked the first invention of the closed loop aquaponic system. Water from a fish tank was trickled into plant beds which then trickled out to recirculate back into the fish tank.

The first commercial aquaponic system was created in the late 1980's, and then in the 1990's two Missouri farmers used gravel beds irrigated by nutrient rich water to grow herbs, vegetables, and tilapia; this was the first time gravel was used in the Aquaponics arena. This system has been duplicated many times over; those same two brothers made a how-to manual that became a staple for many home based aquaponic farms.

Research continues to study how to use this system most effectively, with the least amount of additional water and highest production of crops and aqua life. A recent study found that the perfect balance of fish to plants has the potential to recirculate the same water over and over within the system. If this is achieved, this system of plant and food cultivation will be the most water efficient food production technology in the world.

There have been several recent developments all over the world encouraging the use of aquaponic systems. In the Caribbean, a program was founded to help residents be less dependent on imported food by supporting home aquaponic farming systems. The products are then sold to tourists, creating this new economy helping the environment and the people of the country.

In Bangladesh, one of the universities has begun a program to create an aquaponic system that produces chemical-free fish and produce while making it cost efficient at the same time.

In the United States, a nonprofit foundation called Growing Power, that employs students and teens to assist in the cultivation of fresh produce and food through Aquaponics. They use their own compost to heat the greenhouses, allowing for the year round production of food for the surrounding community. Whispering Roots is another nonprofit that uses aquaponics, hydroponics, and urban farming to provide food to economically disadvantaged populations.

This practice that finds its roots in ancient cultures continues to inspiring farmers to grow "outside the box" with eco-friendlier and self-sufficient systems. As the world of aquaponics grows, it is clear that the method and production will only increase in efficiency and environmentally clean practices.

Chapter 4: Aquaponics Basics

What is Aquaponics?

Aquaponics is the combination of more traditional food production methods and uses both aquaculture and hydroponics in order to grow food naturally for personal consumption. Aquaculture uses tanks and ponds for raising aquatic animals mainly for the purpose of human consumption, while hydroponics refers to the system of growing plants in water instead using the more traditional method of soil-based gardening.

Aquaculture is based on raising fish while hydroponics is based on raising vegetables in water. Aquaponics uses both methods to provide the essential elements for each to be successful.

One of the best features of aquaponics is the inherent benefits it contains in providing protein and vegetables for a well-balanced food source - all at the same time. Not just an excellent way to grow food, but aquaponics is a perfect example of the ultimate recycling program as well!

The process of aquaponics starts with a water tank containing live fish which are fed as often as needed or recommended. The water from the fish tank is then periodically directed to the vegetable growing beds. The water then filters through the plants that are growing and drains slowly from the bottom of the growing beds and is re-directed to the fish tanks.

This works so well because the water from the fish tank contains bacteria from fish waste products combined with uneaten fish food which supplies the growing plants with the nutrients they need in order to grow well. As the fish tank water drains through the growing plants, it is purified and oxygenated and then returned to the fish holding tanks. This oxygen-rich water is needed for optimal fish growth which in turn produces more nutrient-filled water for the plants and the cycle continues indefinitely.

Types of Aquaponics Systems

The aquaponics system can be utilized in ways big and small. Your first experiment can be contained in a miniature system as small as an aquarium inside a tiny apartment gradually increasing in size when more space is available. (This makes it an ideal science experiment to try with the children in your life.)

The size of your chosen system would depend not only on how much space you could devote to it in the right environment, but also be dependent upon how much of your nutritional needs do you want it to fill. The larger amounts of food you want to produce, the larger aquaponics set-up you need to use in order to do so. The versatility in size is most helpful if you are merely interested in seeing if aquaponics is something you might want to become more committed to achieving as a regular part of your daily food supply. While very little food can be produced in a system as small as an inside aquarium, it will give you at least a general idea of what it would take to grow food on a larger scale.

The aquarium method of aquaponics and the larger methods discussed below are very similar except for the size of the tanks — but the process and details are the same. This section will continue explaining the details of the Solar Pond method but understand the details are almost identical for a small aquarium set-up just on a much smaller scale.

Solar Pond System

The Solar Pond system is designed for homes that do not have a lot of space to spare for an aquaponic system thus compacts the typical systems into a method that requires the use of only one tank with the growing bed for vegetables floating as the lid of the tank.

When using this method, the choices for which vegetables can be grown successfully are limited. Tomatoes and/or lettuce are the vegetable most often recommended when using the Solar Pond method. The plant bed is designed to float on top of the water, but a mesh liner must be placed between the plants growing and the fish below since the fish enjoying eating the plant leaves if they are accessible. Talk about situational thievery!

Using this method does not call for pumping or directing the fish tank water into the plant bed as it is floating on top of the water itself. The plants will still purify and enrich the water with oxygen for the fish, and the fish will still provide nutrients for the water the plants are using through their roots in order to grow while the rest of the plant is exposed to the needed sunlight.

Sometimes this method is also called the "raft method" since the plant bed is essentially a floating raft. As the plants grow larger within the floating bed, they can be transplanted to the outer edges of the tank and grow well there leaving the floating bed available for the smaller and more fragile starter plants.

Ranch Tank System

Another method of utilizing aquaponics is the "hole" method that is sometimes called the "ranch tank" method. This system is mostly used by those who are mainly interested in cultivating and harvesting fish and is usually found on regular farm or ranch land.

It consists of a large hole that has been filled with water then supplied with "fingerling" fish which are just small versions of whatever fish you prefer to eat. This is a "closed system" meaning that almost everything needed is provided through nature at nature's timing which does not always cooperate with the timing of the needs for the aquaponic system.

This method is limited by the amount of food it can produce and varies as much as the weather does in any area. The ranch tank does not use pumps to send and return water to and from the plant beds nor does it have any artificial aeration or filtration systems instead depending on oxygenation from occasional rain showers.

This system will eventually cause algae to grow on the surface that can be eaten by the fish in the pond, but it is impractical for growing vegetables because of the difficulty of creating and maintaining a floated plant bed on top of a large artificial pond. The majority of plant growth on the surface of the ranch tank is inedible for human consumption but the fish within the tank will thrive on it thus making it ideal for those who want to use the aquaponic system mainly for harvesting fish for their diets, and not vegetables.

Large Home Production System

The most productive aquaponic system to use for adequate food supply is the main one usually referred to when speaking of an aquaponic system in general and it is comprised of a large fish holding tank(s), elevated growing beds, and a water system for sending water back and forth between the tanks and the beds.

These larger systems often have a filter as well that will separate out large solids from the fish tank water before it is sent to the growing beds. If seriously desiring to provide a good portion of daily nutritional needs through an aquaponic system, this is the type of system you need to use.

One of the best features of the set-up for this larger system is the control you have over what happens during every part of the cycle. You have full control over how much water is sent to the growing beds, how often, the draining methods, etc. All of these variables can be continually adjusted as desired for weather conditions or to increase the speed of growth or for periods of time you may not be able to daily attend to the care of the fish and plants such as when on vacation, etc.

Adjusting the Water Flow

The ability to experiment with adjusting the water flow in your aquaponic system is very helpful in allowing the system to adapt to any part of the country regardless of weather conditions and humidity levels. This can be especially beneficial in times of drought when it is difficult to keep traditional gardens watered adequately as well as provide the water for protein food sources such as cattle.

By the same token, it is also necessary to adjust the water flow for times of high humidity and rainy days in order to avoid root rot in the plants you are growing. Aquaponics can be one of the wisest ways to grow food simply because the water flow can be continually adjusted to meet environmental needs in ways that are not always readily available for traditional crops. While crops grown in the ground can be destroyed through flooding or droughts, plants growing in the aquaponic system can remain healthy in the same scenarios merely by adjusting the water flow within the system.

There are three main ways to adjust or control the water flow within your system: hourly, continuously, or through draining method adjustments. The hourly and continuous methods require the use of a water pump with the hourly method also needing a timer for the water pump. The draining method usually operates without a pump or timer, but requires more involvement from the grower. All three methods can be adjusted in various ways to fit your circumstances, environmental needs, and financial capabilities. The draining method is cheaper since it does not need a pump or timer, but the hourly or continuous methods are easier since they need less daily supervision and/or physical involvement from you.

Automatic Timed Water Flow

Setting the water pump to operate on an hourly basis will allow your system to work intermittently throughout the day by sending set amounts of tank water to the growing beds once every hour. This method calls for the draining holes beneath your growing beds to remain open at all times slowly draining the water back to the fish holding tanks.

The timer on the water pump is usually more flexible in allowing the hourly recommendation to be adjusted to account for the environmental changes often experienced throughout the growing season from weather patterns, etc. For example, if your forecast calls for a lot of rain during the upcoming week, you can adjust the timer accordingly. It also works well for those unable to monitor their systems everyday because of traveling, vacations, work schedules, location, family responsibilities, etc.

Continuous Water Flow

Using the continuous method for watering requires a water pump but not a timer since the pump is working continuously sending a constant flow of water to the plant beds. Since no timers are needed for turning the water pump on and off and need for setting the amount of water being directed to the plants, it could be the "fix it and forget it" water control for aquaponic systems.

But while this method may seem to be the easiest one to use needing the least amount of supervision or input from you, it does not work well for growing anything but very strong plants. The continuous friction of water movement is too strong for the more fragile plants to be able to survive without destroying their tender roots and leaves. Since the constantly flowing water causes a decrease in the oxygen available to the plants' roots, this method also carries a much higher risk of root rot and is not usually the best choice for most systems.

Draining Method of Water Flow

The third method of controlling water flow is referred to as the "draining" method and is similar to the first method because it also makes use of the draining holes beneath the plant beds for operation.

What is different in this method is the process of delivery used to send tank water to the growing beds. It does not use a water pump but instead calls for you to "flood" your growing beds periodically by adding more water to the fish-holding tank until it over flows causing the excess water to be directed to the plant beds essentially flooding them for a little while. The drain holes for the growing beds are temporarily closed while being flooded and then re-opened to allow the draining process to begin slowly draining the floodwaters back to the holding tanks.

But in order for this method to work efficiently while avoiding root rot at the same time, it is extremely important that you allow the roots of the plants growing in your aquaponic system to dry slightly before the next flood cycle. You will need to experiment in order to determine the amount of water that is best to use for flooding as the water eventually returns to the holding tank and can create a continuously flooding situation if too much water is used.

Keep in mind that the growing beds will use up a good portion of the water, and some of it will be evaporates as well depending on the weather and temperatures which are helpful for avoiding this very problem. But it will take a little bit of the trial-and-error process to figure out what works best for your system and environmental conditions.

Miscellaneous Tips

1. Aquaponics is a food production system excellent for use in providing safe and nutritional food for your family without the use of dangerous pesticides and other chemicals that are destructive to the body.

2. This system is used to provide protein through raising fish to eat as well as vegetables to supplement your regular diet and can eventually a good portion of your daily nutrition needs.

3. Aquaponics can be practiced or experimented with using fairly inexpensive

and simple ways before committing the time and resources for creating a system that produces an adequate amount of protein and vegetables for your family's consumption.

4. An aquaponic system can be small enough to fit in the backyard of the average home but can also be expanded as desired to produce greater amounts when the space is available for doing so on a farm or ranch, etc.

5. It is a good place to start when concerned with the level of toxins consumed when using commercial food sources in every-day life.

6. Aquaponics is great for getting your children to happily participate or at least cooperate when you are attempting to gradually feed your family using healthier and organic methods

7. Utilizing aquaponics for yourself can be considerably less expensive than buying the same foods from your local farmer's market or other organic sources.

8. Knowledge and experience in operating an aquaponic system can prove to be a vital tool for survival in crises such as economic collapse, poverty, wartime, etc.

9. You do not need a "green thumb" to successfully operate an aquaponic system!

10. Aquaponics does not use soil at all thus no knowledge of optimal soil ph balances is necessary for success.

11. The use of aquaponic systems for food production does not have to be an all-or-nothing situation. You can downsize or expand depending on your own needs and space available.

12. You can use aquaponics to eventually be your main source of food, or you can use aquaponics to supplement your preferred food sources.

13. Aquaponics does not destroy, pollute, or in any other way damage the environment using chemicals that are often a part of most food sources.

14. Aquaponics will not strip the soil of essential nutrients as occurs with traditional soil-based methods of crop growing.

15. Aquaponics is a perfect example of "green living" using methods of recycling in the best ways possible.

Chapter 5: What Is Aquaponics?

Aquaponic gardening is a system of food production that combines aquaculture and hydroponics. Aquaculture is the process of raising aquatic animals such as fish, prawns, crayfish, or snails in tanks. Hydroponics is the process of cultivating plants in a symbiotic environment, in water.

The availability of high-quality fish has been decreasing over the last several decades. Overfishing, habitat destruction, and ecological damage have decreased the overall number of fish available for American consumption. As a result, fish farms started springing up to manage the decrease in the fish population. These fish farms became experts in aquaculture, the rearing, and cultivating aqua-life, primarily fish.

Soon, fish farms became the fastest growing food industry in the world. Aquaculture farming is much like farming used for chicken and beef; large water systems and pools are full of water and fish. Fish farms are also used for bait, growing algae, and supplying fish and plants for pet stores and aquariums. It can also increase the population of a fish that has become endangered or threatened by extinction.

The different forms of aquaculture include fish farms, mariculture, algaculture, and integrated multitrophic aquaculture; each one of these systems produces different products and provides different uses. Mariculture is the cultivation of animals or plants that require a saltwater environment. Examples of these types of products include many types of shellfish, finfish, like flounder, and sea plants, like seaweed. This type of system is set up in the ocean, where the environment is already perfect for the organisms, with large nets or tanks put in the ocean water, or in tanks outside the ocean filled with saltwater.

Fish farms are the most common form of aquaculture, and the purpose of this system is to create fish for human consumption. About half the world's fish consumption comes from fish farms; this industry has tripled in the last twenty years. The most common fish produced in fish farms are salmon, catfish, trout, cod, and tilapia. There have been several recent legislative acts created to regulate the booming industry.

Algaculture is the cultivation of algae, such as phytoplankton and seaweed. These types of products are created for fish food, feed for other animals, nutritional supplements, and for human consumption. This particular type of system is complicated to oversee, primarily the small algae, which is susceptible to small changes in the environment. Algae require specific lighting, temperature, and nutrition. There are two types of systems used to cultivate algae: open-pond systems and closed-pond systems. Open pong systems are primarily used because they are generally easy to construct, less expensive, and typically produce the most product. However, controlling for light and temperature is difficult. Closed-pond systems are similar to open pond systems, but they control both light and temperature. This type of system produces less product because it is usually smaller and more challenging to build. There are variations of different closed and open-pond systems; however, we won't cover this topic as in-depth.

Lastly, the integrated multitrophic aquaculture system is a more advanced system incorporating many different species into one system. The excrement from one species can be used as fertilizer for another species; for example, shellfish get their nutrients from shrimp and fish droppings.

It is essential to understand the necessary components, and how they work in aquaculture (or for our purposes in an aquaponic system) before starting a complex environment like this system. The purpose of this system is balanced; you are creating a symbiotic relationship where both species benefit from each other's presence.

Understanding the components of the aquaponic system will help you better understand how the system works. Now that you know a little about aquaculture allow me to give you a brief overview of hydroponics. Hydroponics is a system of growing plants without soil, in sand, gravel, and water. There are several different systems within each course; however, the most enormous difference between them is the medium used to house the plants.

Plants suspended in water without a growing medium is called "nutrient film technique." This technique was discovered by Dr. Alan Cooper in the 1960s at the Glasshouse Crops Research Institute in the U.K. This technique comprises plants suspended in plastic material. The plant roots fall into shallow water with a flowing water system flowing to each plant. Nutrients are added to the water that is then dispersed to each plant in the system. This is very popular because of its simple design and inexpensive setup. Small, and generally fast-growing, plants are best for this kind of approach.

Do not let these "simple" systems fool you; although they are simpler to set up, this does not mean they are necessarily "easy."

However, many websites tell you how to build these systems and how to set up water flow, as well as kits that include all the materials you need to start your own.

Fewer nutrients are used for this system because of the flow of water within the system and the recirculation of the water; this system also allows for effortless temperature control. Additionally, these systems do best in a greenhouse environment, getting a lot of sunlight, or in an inside room with artificial light.

From these two systems, aquaponics was born. This system was first used hundreds of thousands of years ago. There is debate about when the system was actually first used; however, evidence suggests it was used in ancient Mexico, where Aztecs used to grow plants on top of rafts in a pond or lake. These rafts comprised a series of "islands" known as "chinampas," a series of canals and rafts using mud enriched with nutrients and channels for water flow.

This was also a widespread practice for cultures in the East, where fish was a significant part of their diet. Even 2,000 years ago, fishmongers in China would sell live fish in baskets and bamboo cages. The rice paddy systems in Asia were also comprised of aquaponic elements; rice paddies floated on the surface of the lake or pond, and fish swam beneath the surface that provided nutrients. In a more advanced aquaponics system, multiple species were used to create a symbiotic relationship. Ducks were housed in cages over the fish ponds, the fish processed the duck droppings in the first pond, the fish in the lower pond lived on the waste that flowed from the first pond, which then flowed into a field with rice and vegetable crops. The water would flow from the first pond down to the crops already fertilized and full of nutrients.

As exploration and trade grew, so did this practice. Fish farming caught on faster. Soon, the fish trade became very popular, which led to one of the first times in history that people experienced overfishing consequences.

Where modern France currently is, the cultivation of oysters was expected and the production of fish for consumption in Italy. Eventually, as trade and transportation became more comfortable, the need for European aquaculture decreased.

The term "aquaponics" was coined in the 1970s. This practice became necessary because fish farmers were trying to figure out how to continue farming fish while not relying on land and water resources. A fisherman's livelihood depended on the amount of fish he could sell. As a result, a system called Recirculating Aquaculture Systems (RAS) was created. This system allowed a large amount of fish in a small space. It produced higher yields while also making a large amount of waste.

At the beginning of the 1970s, research began to study the use of plants to filter fish waste. Dr. James Rakocy, at the University of the Virgin Islands, was the primary researcher identifying how plants could be used in an aquaculture system. The 1980s marked the first invention of the closed-loop aquaponic system. Water from a fish tank was trickled into plant beds, which then trickled out to recirculate back into the fish tank.

The first commercial aquaponics system was created in the late 1980s. In the 1990s, two Missouri farmers used gravel beds irrigated by nutrient-rich water to grow herbs, vegetables, and tilapia; this was the first time gravel was used in the aquaponics arena. This system has been duplicated many times over; those same two brothers made a how-to manual that became a staple for many home-based aquaponic farms.

Research continues to study how to use this system most effectively, with the least amount of additional water and the highest production of crops and aqua life.

A recent study found that the perfect balance of fish to plants can recirculate the same water over and over within the system. If this is achieved, this system of plant and food cultivation will be the most water-efficient food production technology in the world.

There have been several recent developments all over the world, encouraging the use of aquaponic systems. In the Caribbean, a program was founded to help residents be less dependent on imported food by supporting home aquaponic farming systems. The products are then sold to tourists, creating this new economy assisting the environment and the people of the country. In Bangladesh, one of the universities has begun a program to create an aquaponic system that produces chemical-free fish and produce while making it cost-efficient at the same time.

In the United States, there's a nonprofit foundation called Growing Power, which employs students and teens to assist in producing fresh produce and food through aquaponics. They use their own compost to heat the greenhouses, allowing for the year-round production of food for the surrounding community. Whispering Roots is another nonprofit that uses aquaponics, hydroponics, and urban farming to provide economically disadvantaged populations.

This practice that finds its roots in ancient cultures continues to inspiring farmers to grow "outside the box" with eco-friendlier and autonomous systems. As the world of aquaponics grows, it is clear that the method and production will only increase in efficiency and environmentally clean practices.

Many nations are actively educating their people on the practice of aquaponics to both increase healthy, clean food supplies and decrease the need to import food.

In Barbados, in particular, they are also encouraged to sell their grown vegetables to tourists to help families increase their income levels additionally.

With more and more people desiring a more self-sustainable lifestyle and/or living off the grid, aquaponics is a popular option. It is a fair use of space and can be adjusted to individual goals and situations. It can be for the person who intends to go large scale on a commercial basis, to the person who lives in a condo, and simply wants this as both an enjoyable hobby with additional to freshly grown, organic vegetables or herbs, and fish.

There are several ways to build a system using items purchased from your local hardware store. My hope is that by gleaning information from various sources, you'll be able to fine-tune what will work best for your specific situation.

Here's an image of some lettuce roots that used a system using Styrofoam as a growing medium. As you can see, the root systems are long, well developed, and supporting healthy plants.

1.1 Creativity in Growing

If you're looking to find new ways of growing with aquaponics, then you're probably faced with a problem. While this type of gardening has its own challenges, sometimes we are faced with ones we just can't avoid. The biggest problem that most aquaponics enthusiasts face is space. You'll need enough space to deal with the tank, the grow beds (if you're using them), equipment, storage, access to water and power, and enough light for plants to grow. It is a challenging task to achieve a comfortable balance. Still, when faced with an environment that isn't conducive to growing plants successfully, sometimes you have to get creative.

Space

If your first obstacle is space, then you're going to need to look at growing upwards. This means creating vertical towers or guttering arrangements that are held above your fish tank. Your fish won't be affected by lower light, and it will help you keep the algae bloom down by shading the tank. Your compromise with such a system is that you're going to be limited to the type of plants you can grow. Plants that have extensive root systems or that require extra stabilization will not work in smaller containers.

While this might seem like common sense, you can also look at different varieties as a way around the problem. For example, if you want to grow tomato plants but just can't give up space for a large grow bed, compromise with a hanging variety that can be grown in guttering instead.

You can also maximize your space by growing your plants strategically. Grow large plants at the back or center of the grow box and grow smaller plants between the others or in front. This provides the opportunity of producing more plants per box than trying to make all the same crops at the same time in each. As long as your system is flooding high enough to saturate the Grow-Bed sufficient to reach all the plants, your only limit is how they are organized and whether you have enough fish to support them.

Light

If you're growing inside or trying to fit many plants together, then lighting can be a problem. To get around this, consider using reflective panels indoors to maximize your light. Reflectors work to bounce any light rays that aren't aimed at

your plants back at them.

They also reflect heat, so if you're working with a system that needs heating (for example, in winter), then you won't be paying as much for heating by using reflectors. Reflectors can work outside, but because the sun's rays are so intense, they are not advised. A strong reflection can burn plants, melt plastic, and set fire to items, all of which can happen with sun rays compared to weaker artificial light.

Water/Nutrients

There really isn't a compromise when it comes to the size of your pump. If there's one thing you should opt to go bigger with, it is the pump. The pump is what pushes water and nutrients around your system, and if it's not strong enough, you'll find that the plants that are further from the water input may not get watered at all, or in a grow bed environment, the water level may not reach the roots. Plants must have water and nutrients, or they will die; there is no compromise. What you can get creative with here is to have two smaller pumps as your system grows and create two smaller systems cycling off a large fish tank. This will also be a cost-effective way of increasing your system without wasting the pump equipment you already have.

Because your fish provide the nutrition, you also can't compromise on the size of your tank. Without enough fish, plants will not get the nutrients they need to thrive. Too many fish and overcrowding can cause disease, death, and fights, depending on your variety. You can, however, compromise on your type of fish. Some fish are much larger than others, and only opting for a smaller array can mean you'll be able to get more fish per tank. This will up your nutrient level in the water. The same can be said for choosing certain varieties of fish over others since they produce more significant amounts of waste.

Heat

While most plants will not need extra heating in an indoor environment, if you want to grow year-round, you'll have to consider heating. Tropical fish species like Tilapia also require heating if you plan on growing year-round in a non-tropical climate. To maximize your heat, insulate the fish tank well and consider adding a reflective cover in summer and a black one in winter if you're growing outside. Black absorbs heat while the reflective surface will direct it away on hot days. You can also help maximize your heat by using reflective panels on your lighting if you're indoors. The problem with this is that it's easy to overheat your plants and your fish, so you'll also need a ventilation system.

The first thing to do when figuring out the best way to grow is to look at what problems you're facing with your space and tackle them accordingly. Let's see a few alternative ways you can set up a system to grow plants well.

Chapter 6: What Is Aquaponics?

Does this name sound very scientific, or is it just me? Incidentally, this hi-tech sounding name carries a very simple meaning: utilizing waste from water creatures to grow plants. So, waste from water animals – or more respectful, aquatic animals - becomes food for plants. Aquaponics is actually one of the ways to optimize the resources available to provide food with invaluable nutrients to people.

Of course, there is something unique about the whole process of growing the plants because you do not need earth, as in soil. In short, in this very unique process, the plants grow in water just like fish do; they call it hydroponics. This hydroponics also sounds very scientific but at least you know hydro is something to do with water; so it will not leave you bewildered.

So this farming technique uses liquid to produce vegetables and suchlike food, just the same way we use water to rear fish. And we are talking of plants that would ordinarily grow on land; the ones referred to as terrestrial plants.

Will any water suffice in aquaponics?

No and yes. Meaning? The water could be from a river, lake or dam, but the most important aspect is the composition of nutrients in that water. Normally you know clean water has just a few minerals that include mainly hydrogen and oxygen, as in H_2O, and those are, obviously, insufficient to grow your vegetables from tender seedlings to the dining table. So, clearly, the water used in aquaponics needs to be richer. And that is where animal refuse comes in.

How animal farming helps in plant farming

Aquaponic lies in between aquaculture and hydroponics. And remember we mentioned that aquaponics utilizes animal refuse as plant food. Now, if you notice, aquaponics and aquaculture have a similar beginning. The aqua part indicates that both deal with water or liquid material. Aquaculture nurtures both water living animals and water living plants in order to produce food; and its geographical zone is broad and varied - including wild habitat like ocean and sea coastal areas. Hydroponics, on its part, deals solely with nurturing of plants in a watery environment that could sometimes have sand or gravel; still for the purpose of producing food. Now the place of mutual benefit is what we are calling aquaponics.

Why marry aquaculture and hydroponics to get aquaponics?

As mentioned above, this is an issue of optimizing the available resources. It is important to keep the cost of production as low as possible if we are to feed the world adequately and in a healthy way.

For example, in hydroponics, it takes a big wallet to be able to supply the plants with all the necessary nutrients. In any case, you have got to buy them. Incidentally, these nutrients can go up to 20 in number, and the only ones that you do not need to buy are the ones that the natural water provides; namely, oxygen, hydrogen and carbon. Just think of the following nutrients that you need to enrich your water when doing hydroponics:

Macronutrients	Micronutrients (Essential Trace Elements)	Other useful minerals
Nitrogen	Chloride	Cobalt
Phosphorus	Copper	Silicon
Potassium	Boron	
Calcium	Iron	
Magnesium	Manganese	
Sulphur	Sodium	
	Zinc	
	Nickel	
	Molybdenum	

Then again, you cannot go on pumping sodium, phosphorous, copper, potassium, chloride, zinc, and all those other nutrients endlessly, and expect the environment to remain still healthy for the plants. Not with the whole process of food synthesis and release of by products by the plants. So, understandably, there is need to periodically flush the systems in order to dispose of waste. These processes not only call for consistent injection of money into the project, but also time.

Then there are the challenges on the part on aquaculture. This one now calls for daily attention: clearing some portions of water as a way of dealing with excess nutrients in the liquid. This is not cheap either, especially when it comes to labor and supply of water; hence, the logic in merging the two farming technologies.

So how, exactly, does aquaponics cost you less to farm?

Here it is. You have your fish in the usual place: tank, pond or such other place. As life continues, the fish are feeding and relieving themselves, because you obviously supply them with food. Do you know what would happen if that water remained intact for long? You would soon lose your fish due to toxicity. But in aquaponics, you have an outlet from your fish habitat, which carries the water with fish refuse to the plants' hydroponic tray. The plants flourish from the richness of that water, and as they consume the nutrients, the water becomes cleaner. That water is soon clean enough for the fish to dwell in; and, at that juncture, it is let back into the fish dwelling. So, in aquaponics, the fish benefit the plants and the plants benefit the fish – all to your advantage.

Chapter 7: The Types Of Aquaponics Systems

There are many different types of systems used in setting up an aquaponics garden. Some of the most common ones used by a lot of backyard gardeners are media-filled beds, NFT (nutrient film technique), and DWC (deep water culture).

Media Filled Beds

These are the simplest and most common aquaponics systems. Containers are cleaned and filled with rock medium, such as expanded clay and other similar materials. Plants are grown in this kind of medium. A pump is used to bring water from the tank where fishes are raised to the media filled beds. Water either runs in a continuous flow over the rocks or floods the media beds, which are then drained at a later time.

For systems using the flood drain cycles, it can be achieved through several means. There are 3 main methods through which this cycle can be achieved - using a timed pump, using an auto-siphon and using a simple standpipe.

Some media-filled bed systems use a timer. It sets when to flood the beds with water from the fish tank by turning on the pump and when to drain it by turning off the pump. A standpipe is placed in the grow beds to control flooding levels.

Flooding and draining the grow beds can also be performed through the use of an auto siphon

Placed within the beds and the pump is allowed to run continuously. The siphon would periodically drain off the water from the grow beds and return them into the fish tank.

A standpipe in the bed and a continuously running pump is also one way to flood and drain.

Pros and Cons

This section covers the pros and cons of this method of aquaponics.

Pros

- This system works great for people who have taken up aquaponics as a hobby.

- You will find that the parts for the system are easily found. They do not cost too much either. You will be able to procure the material with ease.

- The size of the system depends on your interest. You can make it a big system or a small system. You will be able to save on a lot of space using this method.

- You will be able to grow different kinds of plants.

Cons

- This system will have to be cleaned on a regular basis

- There may be areas in the entire system, which have become anaerobic.

Nutrient Film Technique (NFT)

This technique is more commonly used in hydroponics but also works well in aquaponics. In NFT, water filled with nutrients (from the fish tanks) is pumped into the plants through small gutters. These gutters are enclosed and the water flows through it in very thin films. The plants are in small plastic cups and their roots are allowed access to the thin films of water for nutrient absorption.

This technique is only recommended for certain plants. Plants like leafy greens would thrive well with NFT. Plants too large for plastic cups and with large and invasive root systems are not recommended for this system. Plants that grow too heavy to hang in plastic cups are also not for the NFT.

Pros and Cons

This section covers the pros and cons of this method of aquaponics.

Pros

- The materials in this system are readily available. You will find the parts for this system in the market with ease.

- The growing conditions for this system are more precise. You will be able to select your plants with ease.

- You will find that you are able to change the media without having to worry about a change in the pH of the water. A change in the pH would prove to be extremely dangerous for the plants in the system.

Cons

- You will have to filter the water on a regular basis. This needs to be done well.

You will find that the fish have died otherwise.

- You cannot have a lot of crops growing in this system. This is because of the conditions that have been set by the system.

Deep Water Culture

This type of system works by floating the plants on the surface and the roots dangle into the water. This is among the more commonly practiced aquaponics technique used for commercial growing. There are various ways to achieve this. Some growers place the plants on foam rafts and allow them to float across a tank continuously filled with water from the fish tank. The water is cycled continuously up to the plants and down into the fish tank.

Chift Pist System

This is one of the most popular DIY aquaponics systems. A sump tank houses water, which is pumped into the tank where the fishes are. As the water is pumped into the fish tank, the water level rises until it overflows. The excess water flows out of the tank and into the grow beds. Water that gets into the grow beds eventually drains off back into the sump tank. An auto-siphon is placed within the grow bed to control the flooding and draining.

Often, growers incorporate an SLO for the chift pist system. An SLO is Solids Lift Overflow. An overflow pipe is installed into the fish tank, which goes down into the base of the fish tank. This will draw up all solids (i.e., fish waste) that settles down at the bottom and draw it up into the grow beds.

There are many advantages to this system. One benefit is that the pump is situated away from the wastes and the fishes. It is located in the sump tank. This way, the pump is able to perform better without disturbing the fishes and agitating the wastes, which can cloud the water. Also, this system allows for consistency in the water level of the fish tank, which lessens the stress on the fishes. This is also the most recommended for tall fish tanks as it makes water circulation and waste removal more efficient.

There are also some downsides to using the chift pist system. There is the need to install additional equipment, which is the sump tank. Also, in order for this to work well, the fish tank or stand should be tall. Also, this system would require a larger area to house the entire setup. Timers are also not possible to use for this system.

Aquaponics systems can be as simple or as complex as the grower prefers. The simplest to start with, especially for those who do not wish to purchase equipment is to set up a regular aquarium. Take a few pieces of polystyrene. Cut a few small holes in it. Insert cuttings of plants like watercress and mint into these holes. Float the polystyrene on the surface o the aquarium water. Place fishes and in an instant, a simple aquaponics system.

Based on years of research and feedback, most aquaponics gardeners consider the flood and drain system as the simplest yet the most reliable of all systems. This system requires a very minimal amount of work for care and maintenance. This is also the most recommended system for beginners.

Chapter 8: Set Your Aquaponic

The First Steps – How to Get to It

Every hobby requires some knowledge and some dedicated time to learn and experience everything. In order to start your own aquaponics system, you must know a few things about the water, the fish, and the plants so you can get the idea of what to expect from your system. Aquaponics is becoming a popular system, and it could solve a lot of problems if it would become more widespread. For example, there are many forums where South Africans are trying to build an aquaponics system, but they run into some great issues—for example, there are no supplies, so they have to order them from overseas. Australia is also going in a good direction: many sites you can find online are made by Australians but are not just for Australians. Naturally, European countries and the United States are riding the growing popularity of aquaponics too, and there are serious communities already, running conventions and conferences to fight their war against the dirt-digging big farmers.

Just recently, aquaponics has started to get a heavy attack from "normal" farmers, who are lobbying to change the standards of organic foods and are kicking out the aquaponics food from this market. They haven't succeeded so far, but the "organic" title of aquaponics food is in jeopardy, and if it loses it, it will become very hard for aquaponics farmers to go mainstream. Now, after this small episode of current events, we should take a look at the steps to success.

The Real First Step – Water, Water, and Water!

To make your aquaponics experiment successful, you have to "make" good water for the fish and for the plants. It doesn't matter who you ask—every group and forum will say that it's imperative to cycle the water and adjust the pH levels to make it suitable for every living thing you plan to put in there. There is a step zero, which covers buying (or acquiring) the necessary elements, such as pumps, pipes, tanks, fish, and seeds. You can wait with the living organisms, because there is no point in concerning yourself with those until your water is properly cycled. Cycling the water could take up to a month, and it's quite common to use aquarium filters, pond water, or aquarium water to speed up the process. You should regularly test the water, so buying a master test kit for freshwater is highly recommended, because with one kit, you can test the pH levels and ammonia levels, along with the nitrite and nitrate levels. If you plan to run faster, you should still wait at least a day or two before adding fish to the tank. To avoid disturbing the fish, you must check the tank for leaks and other physical problems before adding them.

In order to start the water cycle or speed it up, you can choose any of the following methods:

Fish feed: You can buy it before you add the fish. The cycle starts when the fish food (which is usually dry worm) starts to dissolve in the water.

Dead meat: Dead fish or crabs are releasing ammonia into the water as they dissolve, and the good bacteria you need feed on ammonia. It's a commonly practiced start method.

Feeder fish: You may start the cycle by actually adding some fish, like goldfish, and growing them a bit before you introduce the actual species you want to raise.

Ammonia: It's possible to add household ammonia. Only food-grade ammonia should be used, and you don't need to add too much to the water.

Fertilizers: Urea fertilizer to be exact. You can get it nearly everywhere, from hardware stores to nurseries, but it requires regular water checking and careful dosing.

Pee: Yes, you can pee straight into the water if you want, but the best way to make it a good starter is to age it a few days somewhere where it can get enough air. Don't do this if you are taking pills or something.

To make the movement of air and water easier, you need to make use of vacuum pumps and standpipes.

Set a standpipe in your system that will ensure the grow bed has enough supply of water. You also need another standpipe at the bottom of the system that will drain out excess and dirty water.

DIY Plans for Standpipes and Overflows

The plumbing to create standpipes and overflows is very simple. Here are some basic plans for components that you can create from parts available at your local hardware store.

The Second Most Important Factor:

Place and Power Putting your aquaponics system in the right place is imperative. You have to consider the light needs of the plants and also keep in mind that fish don't like sun. When you design or buy a system, you will want it to be easily accessible, and to have access to power, without the need to rewire the whole area.

In most cases, beginners tend to place their hydroponics system in their backyard. On its own, it's not an issue, but in order to avoid later problems, you should keep a few things in mind. If you don't want your fish to die out, and you don't want your plants to be weak, you must find the right place for them. For the plants to properly grow, you need at least five to six hours of sunlight. You should inspect your garden and find out which area is the shadiest and which is the sunniest. You have to find a sunnier area that is close to a shadier spot (or where there is a tree), because your fish don't need that much sunlight. Also, direct sunlight warms up the water, which helps algae grow, and that's something you don't want.

To make your aquaponics fish and vegetable farm more sustainable, you have to make it easily accessible for maintenance, and it must have a proper way to receive power. You don't want to buy tens of meters of cord, so this has to be considered during planning. When you place the system and set up the power, you should also keep in mind that it has to be put in a place where it can't get wet, but you can still access it. Also, don't attach it to the growing bed, because the plants might grow over it, and you won't be able to access it without hurting the plants. It's strongly recommended that you make the whole system easily accessible, which includes access to the grow bed and the fish tank too. Taking into consideration the sun's seasonal differences is also important, especially if you plan to run your system in the winter too. Strong weeds and heavy blossom and flower powder isn't exactly beneficial, so you should either cover the ground with cement, bricks, or gravel, or kill all weeds in the area a few weeks before building the system. If you have a tree nearby, make sure that its leaves, flowers, and fruits don't fall into the fish tank, because it could contaminate the water and ruin the whole system.

The Growing Medium

If you are familiar with hydroponics, you've probably seen the different types of medium. Most of them are applicable for aquaponics systems, but since the water is going back to the fish tank, there are several things you should watch out for. Not necessarily because of the water recycling, but for plants' root systems, the size of particles or rocks is important. You should choose nut- or peanut-size medium, preferably from a type that's somewhat porous. Your plants' roots need to breathe, and you want them to expand easily if needed.

The best growing medium for aquaponics are expanded clay pebbles, pea gravel, and riverbed stones. If you don't plan to build a too strong support system for your plants, you should choose the expanded **clay pebbles**—they're cheap and weigh way less than rocks. Clay pebbles are varied in size, and they let the roots breathe, while they are also porous and somewhat sterile. If you plan to use natural clay, you should rinse it with vinegar to clear it and get the idea about its pH level. Visible bubbling means high pH levels, which mean you should look for another medium. Clay pebbles could be bought at several stores, and they are easy to obtain from online stores. Test the clay pebbles, because if they are too soft, you might end up like a guy from one of the forums: his pebbles floated on the water and literally swallowed the plants when the bed got flooded! You need pebbles that have small holes on their surface so the water can flow through them, this way stopping them from floating.

Another good choice of media is rock. It comes naturally, especially if you live near rivers, lakes, or the sea. If not, there is still a high chance to find a natural source for yourself. You should look for round rocks so you can avoid accidents: you cut yourself, or the rock's edge cuts the plant. Since rocks are much harder than expanded clay pebbles, you have to build a strong support for them, and it won't be easy to fill the beds either. Disregarding the source, you should do the vinegar test with rocks too—heavy bubbling means high pH, but it also cleans the rock. After you rinse with vinegar, rinse with water, wait for it to dry, then do another vinegar test, because it might have been only the remnants of the soil or water that caused the bubbling.

In case you are planning to grow your plants starting from the seed, you should consider another media, because the rocks and the clay pebbles won't protect the seed from flowing away. The experience of hydroponics gardeners is invaluable, because you can learn a lot from them. Tiffany from the No Ordinary Home Stead, for example, uses **Rockwool cubes,** which is a very basic and easily obtainable material. You can buy them in hydroponics shops usually, but if you don't want to use Rockwool, simple **cotton wool** is good enough, though you can't install it in the system. We used to do germination experiments in school. We put cotton wool in the bottom of a cup, put the seeds on it, and poured in just enough water to keep the cotton wet. If it was kept in a warm, somewhat dark place, after a week or so, we would have a strong germinated seed, and after another week, it was ready to plant in soil. You can do this too.

The Fish

So what do we have? We know how to test the water, how to cycle, where and how to place our system, and which media (if we plan on using media) we should use. Now, there are two things we should take a look at so you can start on the journey of having an aquaponics garden fully armed with knowledge: the living parties, **the fish and the plants**. Let's start with the fish, because they are the most important part. Remember, you can only grow plants if your fish are happy. Fish provide the power to the whole hydroponics system—without them, there is no nutrition so the plants die of starvation. There are hundreds of experimental aquaponics systems out there, and apart from fish, many people try to add lobster, clam, and crayfish to their fish tank, with various outcomes.

One of the most exciting experimental fish I have read about is the Giant Snakehead (Channa Micropeltes). It's common near Asia, and a guy in South China added it to his hydroponics system. He also raises tilapia and shrimp, so he has some crazy ideas. It looks like his experiments are successful, because his Giant Snakehead is quite big now, about 9–10 inches, which is great considering that it could grow up to 50–60 inches.

You shouldn't start your adventure with tropical or even exotic fish. The temperature is the most important factor you must consider when it comes to choosing the right fish. It's best to choose an edible fish species, which appears naturally in your area, because it means that it's already adapted to your temperature. Since aquaponics means that you have a fish farm, you have to check the regulations in your jurisdiction, and it won't hurt to check in with the fishing and gaming office in the area. Let's see the most common fish types raised in aquaponic gardens:

Trout

Tilapia

Catfish

Carp (also goldfish and koi carp)

Silver perch

Apart from actual fish, you can also use crayfish and other crustaceans, and freshwater moss could help the plants' roots clear the water.

When you plan to raise fish, you have to take into consideration the numbers too. Mentioning this to aquaponics gardeners will show you that there is no actual recipe, nor any kind of real consent about it. You can raise the stocking levels as high as they are in an aquaculture system, but high density raises the odds of issues coming up eventually. High fish density also requires monitoring and keeping the optimum water conditions all of the time, which practically takes away the comfort aquaponics should actually grant. The usually suggested rate is ten to twenty fish per 500 liters of growing media, but it depends on the feeding rates, the pumping rate, the species, and several additional factors. However, with only ten per 500L, you can't go wrong, though adding a few fish won't hurt, as long as there is enough water, food, and bacteria to break the wastes, and enough plants to clean the water properly.

As a basic principle, you have to feed your fish with good-quality pellet—the best proven is the one they use at fish farms. You can use larvae, maggots, and worms as supplements, but it's recommended to use them only as complementary food, so you should keep a fine pellet at hand. You don't need to keep your aquaponics system in a completely closed loop. It is not a must to solely rely on the products of your own system and feed the fish with scraps and rubbish. Regarding the amount of food you should give to your fish, there is one simple rule: give them as much as they want to eat. Grab a spoon, add the food slowly, and see how much remains after each spoon of food you add. This takes a few minutes, but overfeeding isn't good, and the uneaten food starts to rot, lowering oxygen levels and increasing ammonia levels.

The Plants You Can Grow in an Aquaponics System

Planting the plants you want to grow is among the easier things to do in an aquaponics system. Nearly everything can be grown with this technique, and if you are patient, you could start the whole action from the very beginning: from the seeds. As I already mentioned, the expanded clay pebbles are not exactly the best media for growing seeds, so you should choose something different like cotton wool or Rockwool cubes. In case your media consists of small pebbles or stones, you might not need additional media to plant seeds with. After a few days of sprinkling the seeds, you will see the seedlings rise up from the grow bed. Those who don't want to worry about whether the seeds are germinating or not should buy seedlings from stores or from the marketplace. In case you buy seedlings, make sure to wash their roots thoroughly (but carefully) from any soil remnants, as it could contaminate the water.

In an aquaponics garden, you can plant the seeds much more closely to each other than in soil-based gardens, so you can have a bigger harvest at a smaller place. When it comes to choosing the plants you can grow in your aquaponics garden, the main point is to choose only stuff you can eat. But nearly everything can live in an aquaponics system. Some people experimented with tomatoes, for example, and they grew really nicely, usually with sand as a medium. Because of the tomatoes' nature (the edible crop is on the roots), you can't grow it in DWC or constant flow, but a flood and drain system with a softer medium is just perfect. I've found several descriptions and galleries featuring trees grown in aquaponics, such as a dwarf peach. These trees are strong, and they yield a fresh, delicious fruit—and a lot of it. I was thinking about trying out berries like currants, blueberries, mulberries, and raspberries in half-barrels, with some stronger medium like a mix of clay pebbles (to hold water) and rocks (to have a firm support for the bushes).

You can have a constant flow of fresh vegetables if you plant the seeds or seedlings periodically so you have seedlings, half-grown vegetables, and mature plants in your system. You can harvest all year long and don't need to buy anything in the stores. Different herbs are also growing well in aquaponics, so you can make your own spice mixes from basil, oregano, and so on.

Chapter 9: Designing A System

Why is Aquaponics a good and simple solutiin for a healthier and natural life?

Aquaponics system offer you the chance to consume recent and organic fishes and vegetables. Your system will offer you up to fifty kilo of fishes and many kilo of vegetables in vi months time!

It is a simple job to create up your own aquaponics system. Your system doesn't want huge area for its institution.

Aquaponics system could be a real cash saver in each its building and its maintenance i.e. you'll got to pay solely the 1/10 of water scrutiny with the classic farming

You can notice aquaponic systems enthusiasts around your own space and round the world. can|they're going to|they'll} be a good facilitate for you once you will arrange to take your initial steps.

Aquaponics systems ar straightforward expandable systems. you'll be able to modify them any time you're feeling love it as an example you'll be able to increase them a lot of components to succeed larger harvest.

The Idea of aquaponics systems came from combination of cultivation and aquicultural Systems. It came because the best solve for the negative sides for each farming and Aquaculture. Aquaculture re-circulating method is concerning obtaining the surplus nutrients out of the system, this can be happening daily normally, by obtaining share of the water out. Then we've got water wealthy in nutrients that require to be disposed and clean H2O needs to replace it.

To feed the plants the aquicultural system wants all the time costly nutrients and additionally on an everyday basis a waste disposal issue seems by flushing the systems.

Aquaponic Systems came because the magic solve for the down sides of each cultivation and farming within the best means, brooding about re-circulating each systems along we are going to notice that the negative facets of cultivation "getting the surplus nutrients out of the system" is that the best solve for the negative aspect of farming "the aquicultural system is in want all the time for costly nutrients" and no a lot of waste water reason for the periodic flushing of the systems meaning no a lot of lost cash. And by the magic bit of aquaponic, we are going to have soldier, vegetables and fruits all the time within the within the most cost-effective and cleanest means.

Aquaponics system provide you with the chance to consume recent and organic fishes and vegetables. Your system will provide you with up to fifty weight unit of fishes and many weight unit of vegetables in six months time!

It is a straightforward job to make up your own aquaponics system.

Your system doesn't would like massive area for its institution.

Aquaponics system could be a real cash saver in each its building and its maintenance i.e. you'll ought to pay solely the 1/10 of water scrutiny with the classic farming.

You can notice aquaponic systems enthusiasts around your own space and round the world. can|they're going to|they'll} be an excellent facilitate for you after you will arrange to take your initial steps.

Aquaponics systems area unit simple expandable systems. you'll be able to change them any time you're feeling adore it as an example you'll be able to increase them a lot of components to succeed larger harvest.

We feed the fishes ordinarily then the fishes extract ammonia into the water. The pump is lifting the water from the marine museum up to the grow-bed.

The water is dripping down through the porous media bed / filter, passing through the roots of the plants before discharging back to the tank.

The plants roots absorb the water and nutrients that they have to grow, improvement the water by this fashion from the nutrients, returning back to the tank recent and clean water that fish would like.

Ok, let's have shut scrutinize the roots of the aquaponics plants, area unit they creating use from the marine museum water because it is, or area unit there hidden secrets behind the aquaponics system success? the solution is not any, there MEasure} hidden troopers operating unceasing at the backstage for the success of the system so; let me introduce you currently the grow-bed microorganism. i do know most people after we hear "Bacteria" (or "Germs" in keeping with the disinfectant commercials) area unit meant to be dangerous, aren't we? No, as each issue else has its sensible and dangerous sides, this type of microorganism is helpful and that we will decision it the most soldier in aquaponics system.

Normally the fish area unit emission ammonia and it's harmful for the fish (big harm to tissues of the excretory organ and gills, shriveled resistance to illness and Weak growth or perhaps death). moldering food additionally creates ammonia. fortuitously there on the surface of the grow-bed media there area unit bacteria genus microorganism, that eat the ammonia and acquire out chemical group (this chemical group has most less dangerous impact on the fish than the ammonia, however still the case has some negative facet that It stops the fish from seizing oxygen).

Luckily there area unit different sensible microorganism "Nitro-bacteria", that eat the chemical group and acquire out nitrate.

Nitrate happens to be the most effective food for the plants, that create them grow therefore quick, that the plants roots absorb the nitrate and water to age quicker than in the other system.

After plants have absorbed all the nitrates, the water is returning recent once more, (free of ammonia or perhaps nitrite) back to the marine museum. this can be what we have a tendency to decision "Aquaponics System atomic number 7 cycle" that is that the real technique, created by the Aquaponics, a true technique for the foremost economical System that's manufacturing cannon fodder and Organic (vegetables / fruits) to each house, and might be turned simply to your home business similarly.

If you're old with farming you're OK. there's no distinction than the conventional approach of growing plants in Aquaponics System the grow-beds will be stuffed with media like expanded clay pebbles, gravel, vermiculite, perlite and lots of different ways that will be used as media to grow the plants, even it will be floating foam rafts that sit on the water surface.

High density of fish will be adult up in AN aquaponics system marine museum. several forms of fish will be breeding in Aquaponics systems like Tilapia, White bass, Crappies, Trout and lots of different species. usually we will say it's a therefore productive fish growing system. selecting the fish you'll be growing depends on several factors, in our Aquaponics Fish facilitate guide, you'll notice all the required information.

A common question that the beginners area unit forever asking: that plants they'll cultivate in AN aquaponics system? Ok we will say that every one the vegetables and herbs will be exhausted the aquaponic farming with no exception, several forms of fruits too, however selecting the vegetables or fruits that you simply are going to be growing in your aquaponics system it'll be represented later in aquaponics farming space.

Aquaponics systems dissent in kind from one system to the opposite, they'll be as easy or as complicated in keeping with your wishes, let's have a glance.

Chapter 10: Building & Operating Your New System

Before you set up your Aquaponics system, there are some things you need to consider carefully. Firstly, where will your system be located? It is key to choose your location before you start building. Aquaponic systems can be incredibly heavy, even small ones, and so, it would be wise to put it together in its final location if possible, rather than putting the system together elsewhere and having to transport it once built.

Another reason for choosing the location first, is to take advantage of all the available space. When considering special requirements, you may, in fact, decide that you have room for a bigger system, but want to start with a smaller one, and you could add extra grow beds and fish tanks further down the line.

Will your system be indoors or outdoors? Indoor systems tend to be built slightly differently to outdoor ones, and different materials are often used. For example, you may want to use a barrel for your fish tank outdoors, whereas inside, you might choose a glass tank that looks smarter and fits in better with your décor! Indoors, you'll also most likely want your grow bed directly above your fish tank, rather than to the side, in order to save space. The weight of your system is also an important consideration, especially when building indoors. You wouldn't want to build it on the second floor of your house, only to walk in one day and find it's landed in your lounge! Indoor systems will also require grow lights, so think carefully about where best to build your aquaponic system.

If you opt for an outdoor build, the ground beneath the system needs to be stable and level. Moreover, because these systems are heavy, if you place it on dry or soft soil, the legs of your system could sink, which can lead to flooding. Concrete slabs are a good base for your system. If you do place your system on grass or soil, concrete or wood under each leg may prevent it from sinking. It is recommended that the fish tank is placed on a base to protect it, and to allow for plumbing and drains to be connected underneath.

When choosing the location for your system, you must consider the access to utilities and electrical sockets for your air and water pumps. Inside, this won't generally be an issue. No matter where your system is, remember, water and electricity don't mix well, so all electrical outlets need to be shielded from water. Ensure that you have purchased a residual-current device (RCD), too. You should also consider ease of access. The system will need daily testing and monitoring, and you will, ideally, need to be able to move around the entirety of it to check for leaks, inspect your plants for insects and check up on the health of your fish. Another consideration is the water source you are using; is your system near enough to a water source so that you can top it up with ease whenever necessary? Where will any wastewater be disposed of? Your system also needs to be in a safe location where it won't get vandalized, or attacked by larger animals such as rabbits or foxes - you may want to put a fence around it to minimize these risks.

The final consideration is the climate in which you live. If the weather tends to be hot all year round, then your system will be fine outdoors. If you have harsh winters, will you not operate it during colder months, or will you place your system in a greenhouse all year round? What are your night-time temperatures like? Will you need a heater at certain times of the day? Extreme environmental conditions shouldn't be taken lightly because they can seriously affect your plants. Snow and heavy rain can cause damage to the system too; for instance, large amounts of rain can dilute the water and even flood the system if you have no overflow mechanism. Rain poses a significant danger to unprotected electrical sockets too. Therefore, it would be smart to protect your system (climate dependent) with some sort of shelter – a greenhouse or shed, possibly. Alternatively, you may want to shut your system down when you know that the rainy or cold season is coming, or move it inside.

It isn't just cold weather that can have an adverse effect on your system; you will also need to consider sunlight vs. shade. Sunlight is quite clearly vital for plants, and they'll need to receive the optimum amount of sunshine each day. Equally, if the sun is too intense, you may need to consider some sort of shade system over the grow beds. For instance, lettuce, cabbages, and salad greens don't thrive in the presence of excessive sun and will flourish better in a shaded area. Other plants can show a slow growth rate if they don't receive enough sunlight hours. Consider where, and when, shadows will cross your grow bed location and arrange your plants accordingly; for example, tall, sun-worshipping plants could be cleverly used to shade low-lying, shade-loving plants.

A greenhouse isn't essential for a home Aquaponic system, but having one can be a solution to many problems. For instance, it can extend the growing period or even allow for year-round production of plants in some areas. A greenhouse will protect the system from elements such as rain, snow, and wind, as well as providing protection from pests, predators, and vandals. Working in them is also comfortable during cooler periods. The frame of the greenhouse can also be useful to encourage plants to climb, or can be used to hang up shading material. However perfect a greenhouse sounds, there are some downsides; for instance, depending on how sophisticated you want your greenhouse to be, the initial purchase cost can be pretty steep.

However, this is where things can get complex and can seem overwhelming for a beginner in aquaponics. The thing is, your plants are not the only thing to take into account; you also need to remember that fish are a key part of your system. The fish tank shouldn't receive direct sunlight and should be placed in the shade. Excessive light causes algae growth (due to photosynthesis). Light also acts as a cue to breed, which can turn some fish species, extremely aggressive. Not ideal. Some growers cover their fish tanks with a removable cover. In addition, try not to place your tank under any overhanging trees, which may drop leaves and other debris into your fish tank, affecting your water chemistry, clogging your pipes, and putting your system at risk of contamination. You also need to be wary of predators! Some may see your fish as a free lunch, so some sort of screening will be needed to protect them.

In Chapters 5 & 6, we'll cover the ins and outs of plants and fish in vast detail - so that you don't miss a trick. It would be devastating to build a fantastic Aquaponics system, only to find that your fish aren't happy, and the plants you want to grow aren't suitable.

There is a close relationship between the size of the grow bed and the size of the fish tank. The quantity of fish excretions dictates how many plants can grow; too many fish, or too much fish food - will result in too much ammonia being produced. If, in this case, the grow bed isn't big enough, there won't be enough bacteria to break this waste down fast enough, and slowly the water will poison your fish. Too few fish, and too many plants, will mean there won't be enough nutrients for all the plants to flourish. Like in all aspects of life, balance is key.

Connecting Up Your System

Whichever type of system you decide on using, it will require various PVC pipes, PVC connections, fittings, tubes, and hoses to create the means for the water to flow throughout the system. You will also need some sort of sealant. Usually, the PVC parts are permanently connected using PVC cement, or they can be temporarily sealed using silicone sealant - assuming the joints aren't under excessively high water pressure. As well as the plumbing components, you will also need tools such as hand saws, hammers, drills, electric saws, pliers, screwdrivers, tape measures, and so on. The pipes and plumbing materials used in your system need to be free from toxins, and any plastic should be food-grade to prevent your system from being contaminated with chemicals. Crucially, all pipes should be black or non-transparent, otherwise, algae may start to grow inside.

In Aquaponics, the sump tank is generally placed lower than your fish tank, and this is where all the equipment needed to keep your fish healthy will be placed; filters, heaters, and so on. To simplify, a pump will force water from the sump tank into the fish tank. As the fish tank fills up, the water flows into the grow beds and later drains back into the sump, before being pumped back up towards the fish tank - continuing the cycle.

To simplify the setup and to avoid having to have a complicated network of pipes (and to reduce the risk of pump failure), a 'Bell Siphon' is often used. With the siphon in place, when the water reaches a certain height, it drains out through the siphon faster than the rate at which the water fills the grow bed. As the siphon drains the water, holes at the bottom cause the siphon to break the suction, and the whole process begins again.

How it works:

Water from the fish tank flows into the grow bed, providing the plants with nutrients.

The water reaches the high mark of the bell siphon and starts to drain into the pipe, causing a vacuum effect, drawing air into the drain pipe too.

With the air removed from the bell siphon, the water flow via the drain increases dramatically, thus water is draining from the grow bed faster than it is being replenished.

The siphon eventually reaches the bottom of the grow bed and starts to suck in air instead of water, which in turn causes the siphon to break, stopping the grow bed from draining, and the cycle begins again.

While bell siphons can be tricky to get right, once you have them working properly, they can be extremely effective.

I'm not going to go into too much more detail with plumbing and connecting your system, as it can be difficult to describe. You will be better placed to select which Aquaponics technique you are going to use, then look at some videos online to help you design your system. The actual ins and outs of how to connect it, depends on the size, shape, and set up of your system, which will all be unique to you.

Cycling

No, I'm not talking about getting your bike out here; system cycling is the term given to the process of first establishing the beneficial bacteria for your system, which is, as you know, critical for the nitrogen cycle and therefore your entire aquaponic garden.

Cycling begins when you first introduce ammonia into your system. You can do this by adding every-day, household cleaning ammonia, but please only use the pure kind; avoid anything that contains soap, perfumes, colorants, or any other type of additive. The bottle should list the ingredients or will be labeled 100% ammonia, pure ammonia, clear ammonia, or pure ammonium hydroxide. If it doesn't have one of these terms, don't use it. A novel way to find out if it is suitable is to shake the bottle - if it foams, it isn't suitable.

Pure ammonia can be purchased in DIY stores, cleaning supply shops, or in supermarkets. If you can't find it locally, you can buy it online. There are other sources of ammonia, and these include Ammonium Chloride, human urine, or even a piece of dead fish! Those last two sources are purely for entertainment purposes, and should NOT be added to your system for obvious reasons. ☐

Whichever source of ammonia you use, add it to your fish tank, then start testing the water until you get an ammonia reading between 2 & 4 ppm. If you have a smaller tank, add only half a teaspoon or less, wait, test, then, if necessary, add more. It usually takes around 5 teaspoons of 100% clear ammonia or half a teaspoon of ammonium chloride powder to give you a reading of approximately 3-4 ppm in 100 gallons of water. If you do add too much, you can drain some of the water, and top it back up with new water, then test it again.

One mistake I see newbies making regularly - is adding ammonia, not seeing an immediate reading, then proceeding to add more. The test still reads zero ammonia, so they add more, then they complain the test doesn't work. If you have a reading of zero ammonia, you may have added too much and actually overwhelmed the system. Start again, dilute with fresh water, and take another reading.

Once you get the optimum ammonia reading, you will need to test your water for ammonia, pH levels, and nitrites every day. I recommend you record these, along with notes, so that you can track any changes. At this point, the pH needs to be between 7.0-7.8. A level higher than this is okay during cycling, assuming that you haven't planted anything yet. Equally, though, I would recommend you try to reduce it, just so that you know how to do it – refer back to Chapter 2 for clarity on how to raise and lower pH.

Once the ammonia levels begin to drop, this is a great sign; this means the nitrifying bacteria are starting to convert the ammonia into nitrites, then into nitrates. Add a small amount more ammonia in to raise the levels back to the 2-4ppm range. Record the nitrate levels, too, as this is the next step in the cycling process.

Your system will be fully cycled once nitrite AND ammonia levels fall to (or close to) zero. Once this has happened, you are ready to add the fish; you will no longer need to add more ammonia because the bacteria will start to be fed via the ammonia excreted from the fish and the fish waste! Take a second to be proud and reflect on how far you have come already.

You are almost ready to start planting seeds too. At this stage, the pH should be between 6.5-7.0, because remember, the plants require a lower pH than bacteria. The entire cycling process can take anywhere from 10 days to 2 or 3 months.

Inoculation

Some growers choose to accelerate the cycling process by inoculating the system. There are a number of strategies here...

Inoculating with store-bought inoculant bacteria at start-up – it costs between $30 - $50, but can save you potentially months of cycling time!

Taking "inoculator plants" from another aquaponics system and adding them to your system – one problem is that you may bring with it - other things from the donor aquaponic system, like duckweed, crawfish eggs, etc.

Adding a water sample of media from another aquaponic system or body of water, and adding it to your fish tank. This is sometimes referred to as 'live water'.

The only difficulty with inoculation is that you need to be confident that the source the bacteria is coming from, is a healthy one. You may know somebody who has an Aquaponics system, or you may not. There is always the off chance that you could borrow water/plants from a grower who has diseased fish in their tank without realizing it. By doing this, you would run the risk of introducing disease to your brand new, clean system! Not ideal.

This method of cycling is known as fish-less cycling. The advantage of starting up your system without adding the fish has some benefits for beginners. Firstly, it is far less stressful for both you and the fish! You are not needing to worry about killing off some of your new fish friends while getting the ammonia levels correct. Second, you don't have to worry too much about pH levels, as you don't yet have any fish or plants.

Cycling is far quicker without fish because you can elevate the ammonia concentration to a far higher level than you would if you had fish. If you have fish in the system when you start it up, it can take 4-8 weeks for it to cycle.

In addition, you can control precisely how much ammonia is in your system; if the ammonia level is high, you can stop adding ammonia for a couple of days and wait for the bacteria to grow and nitrites to be introduced. Or, you could remove some water out and dilute with fresh water. It's hard to do this when you have fish in the water because this may throw off the temperature levels.

Once the cycling process has completed, you should add all your fish at once, as opposed to adding them gradually. If using carnivorous or aggressive fish, this can be better because they are far less likely to attack each other if they are introduced together; sometimes, they can be territorial if a number of them are introduced at a later date. For more detailed information regarding fish, don't fear, because Chapter 5 is up next!

Finally, you are ready to plant your seeds. Surprisingly, it is advisable that you start with seedlings when your system is first up and running. Once you have plants established and your system has been running successfully for at least three months or more, then you can start adding seeds as well. For more information on plants and seeds, see Chapter 6.

Chapter 11: Troubleshooting:

Repairing Your Fishy Business

Plant Wellbeing: Help, my crops are ill!

Plants within an aquaponic system are not as likely to suffer with ailments and deficiencies compared to crops at a garden. But, they could still pose with the signs of a sickness. If only a couple of plants seem unhealthy, they could be diseased. But if all your plants seem unhealthy, and especially if this happens more slowly, it's probably a system issue.

Deficiencies

Plants may suffer from deficiencies, typically denoted by inferior growth and fruit set, or discoloration of the leaves. Deficiency is frequently reminiscent of a pH problem -- it isn't that the nutrients are not there, but the crops can't get them. If pH is at an acceptable variety, nutrient deficiencies ought to be treated as summarized below. Deficiencies are more prevalent in recently established systems. A number of the most Frequent deficiencies include: Nitrogen lack

Yellowing of leaves, starting at the borders. Boost system input to fix this dilemma.

Potassium lack

Poor flowering and fruit set; yellowish veins. Supplement with potassium hydroxide for fundamental systems or potassium carbonate for systems that are acidic.

Calcium lack

Poor fruit collection; blossom end rot; burnt hints; leaf curl. Insert calcium carbonate; include a quart (liter) of crushed egg shells, sea shells, coral or limestone into the machine.

Iron lack

Yellow veins; leaves from yellow to white. Supplement with chelated iron to readily figure out this matter.

Infection

Even though more rare in aquaponic units than in gardens that are normal, plants may suffer from illness. In the event of symptoms like fungal spores, mildews or spotting on the leaves inexplicable by temptation, eliminate and destroy all affected crops whenever possible to stop additional contamination. Avoid planting veggies for the identical household for 6-8 weeks if possible.

Since aquaponic systems don't have dirt (which is actually the selling point of aquaponics), we must take care of some amount of nutrient deficiency. Nutrient deficiency usually happens when you give your fish poor-quality fish feed. I understand -- we would like to decrease operating costs as far as possible. But when your plants and fish endure, the cost-cutting you are doing will not create a lot greater yield of investment. It's much better to put money into high quality fish feed and allow nature create a nutritious bounty of fish and vegetables to you.

In the last evaluation, you will still save money when your machine is up and functioning easily. And remember: garden aquaponics is about providing clean meals to your loved ones. Your garden aquaponic system won't be able to do so in case the only source of nourishment isn't sufficient to fulfill the requirements of these fish and plants. But if nutrient deficiency continues despite changes in the fish diets, then look at adding mineral supplementation into the water. Check with an agricultural pro so it is possible to get some insight about which particular particular minerals that your plants will need to live in an aquaponic system. Always talk to an agricultural pro before adding anything into the water. Bear in mind, everything that enters the water impacts not just the fish, but also your crops and all of the beneficial bacteria in water. If one definite supplementation destroys the beneficial bacteria in the water, then your own body will fold and fall!

Healthy crops, no fruit

Nitrogen creates lush, healthy, green leaves, also is very important to plant development. But, too much nitrogen can cause crops to create a lot of healthy foliage at the expense of fruit and flowers. In case you've mastered a calcium or potassium deficiency and also have healthy looking plants, but no fruit, then you could get a surplus of nitrogen from the system. Dilute the machine water, then reduce inputs, develop leafy greens rather than fruiting crops or add more plants into the machine. If you're growing in a place where bees are rare, a collapse to fruit may also be the effect of a lack of pollination. In cases like this, you'll have to hand pollinate your plants to accomplish fruit collection.

Often asked questions

My plants are wilting and dying. What is wrong with my machine?

A: wilting plants might be brought on by extremely high or extremely low ph levels. Check the ph level of your own water and inspect the tolerable ph level to your plant types on your expansion beds. In case you've got a constant flow system set up, the origins of these plants might not be getting adequate oxygen. Try switching to a formerly hourly system or ebb-and-flood system rather. When it does not work, consider nurturing another kind of vegetable and see whether the new seedlings endure the increase bed. Pests may also lead to wilting so be watching out for big pests and tiny bugs which might not be immediately evident to the naked eye.

When in doubt, speak to an aquaponic expert in your area and consult him/her. When it is not wintertime along with your crops are suddenly showing signs of impending death, the nutrient levels in your water might not be sufficient. You're able to immediately remedy this issue by incorporating more fish feed into your holding tank. But, increasing fish feed can lead to cloudiness on your holding tank, so ensure you shell out the water regularly. If everything else fails, draining the tank partly and refilling it with clean, no chlorinated water can help clean the effluents.

It is wintertime here along with my plants are wilting.

A: in case you've planted native fruits and vegetables on your mature beds, then the issue is probably plant nourishment. Throughout winter, all creatures (with the exception of the polar bear(possibly) proceed more slowly due to their diminishing surroundings temperature. When fish proceed more gradually, they need less food. With less food, you've got less ammonia from the water and crops want the ammonia so as to survive. To improve this circumstance, you may opt to bring some warmth to the tank to promote the fish to be lively. After the fish become more energetic, look at adding more fish feed so that the effluent level in the water increases. If it fails, you don't have any option but to decrease the amount of crops at the mature beds.

The leaves of the plants are turning yellow or brownish for no reason whatsoever

A: yellowing or browning leaves are characteristic signs of toxicity. Sometimes, the noodle soup has been pumped to the grow beds might have elevated levels of minerals too large for crops to endure. Plants are incredibly sensitive to substances. Plant tissue succumbs almost instantly to elevated levels of nutrient salts from the soil. The identical thing occurs whenever there's a high degree of mineral salts from the water. Inversely, yellowing or browning of leaves can also signal nutrient deficiency. In these circumstances, add more fish feed into the tank to boost the nutrient levels in the water being cycled into the increase beds.

I see aphids eating my plants!

A: regrettably, this is mother nature's way of feeding aphids. Insects don't discriminate between wild-growing veggies and vegetables that are cultivated so it's necessary to care for this aphid invasion instantly. There are just two ways which you may manage this issue without resorting to pesticides. Your first solution is to plant veggies which will attract valuable creatures like lady bugs. The woman bugs will look after the aphids for you. This is a fantastic long-term solution but regrettably, it might not work when you've got an extreme aphid invasion onto your palms.

The next solution is to obtain a bunch of mature lady bugs out of the regional agricultural source or plant nursery. Now, be cautious when introducing female bugs into your beds. Odds are, you will find ants nearby. Aphids and rodents have a symbiotic (mutually beneficial) relationship and so, whatever threatens the aphids will be taken care of from the more powerful and meaner ants. It'll be best to present valuable insects during the day when insect activity is usually lower.

I see caterpillars munching on my veggies!

A: again, this is simply nature's way of ingesting the 'young ones'. You do not need to worry to the caterpillars. If you're able to produce a homemade garlic spray, then use that. Otherwise, simply wear your gloves and pick off the caterpillars. Do not squish the bugs however! Instead, place the caterpillars into a jar with a few leaves so you are going to have some live food to your fish. In this manner, nothing is wasted and you have the ability to turn the tables.

My plants appear to be stunted.

A: this is quite probably nutrient deficiency. Check one of these answers mentioned above. If none of the options operate, check the ph level of the water. If the water is too bloated, which could possibly be the origin of the slow development of your prized crops.

The water level at the holding tank is obviously below the optimal amount.

It might be milder this time of the year or your crops are increasing at a quicker speed. In any instance, simply add more water. Ensure the water was de-chlorinated. You might even put in a booster dose of pond water to make certain the bacterial population in the water stays steady. Water reduction of over fifty percent in one holding tank system might necessitate cycling of germs.

The water within my system is very dirty and there are a whole lot of floating effluents from the water. I can hardly see my fish!

This is a terrible situation as your fish could die in a matter of days when the water has become so polluted. The most usual cause of contaminated water within an aquaponic installation is a lot of fish foods being inserted into the water. If that isn't true, then the buffer (press) and the filtration mechanism aren't performing well. It's possible to add an extra filtering mechanism into the return to wash out the water. Any cleared waste out of the water has to be removed manually. Don't return filtered waste into the machine since this will induce the water once more.

There is a thin coating of ice in addition to the holding tank.

The weather has finally gotten the better of your own body. Look at heating the holding tank and then installing added'bubble manufacturers' to make mini-currents from the tank. The excess water motion will help reduce the incidence of ice formation on the surface of the water. However, before you do one of these measures, check if your fish are still living!

There is discharged from the water, even when water was cycled satisfactorily a couple weeks before.

There needs to be no foaming in based aquaponic systems. The most usual cause of foaming is family detergents. Household detergents might have been introduced if you'topped off' the tank with much more water. To cure this issue, drain fifty percent of their water content of this holding tank and include de-chlorinated water. Continue doing so daily before the foaming goes off.

There are dead fish floating in the tank.

Eliminate the dead fish immediately. An aquaponic system isn't meant to manage dead fish -- that the surplus of ammonia will conquer the system and might also result in increased fish mortality.

All of the fish are almost dead but are still gasping for air.

A: there is no use in prolonging the misery of fish. Aquaponic farmers usually only flatten the minds of nearly dead fishes. This is actually the only method to eliminate the fish. Should you allow the fish perish in the holding tank, then the water is only going to be polluted.

Fish from the holding tank aren't acting normally; a few are swimming some aren't eating well.

If this is the very first time to boost these fish species, so you might have given the fish the wrong kind of food. Consider switching brands.

Fish appear to be clubbed in the surface of the water.

The oxygen amount in the water is inadequate to support all of the fish. Insert extra aeration mechanism to maintain the water well oxygenated. This should take care of the issue.

Fish are leaping out to capture insects which are hovering close to the surface of the tank.

The simplest way to take care of feisty fish would be to put in a display in addition to the tank.

I see red worms from the tank!

Do not be worried about the red worms. If it is possible to collect the worms, then do this. You now have free, live food to contribute to a own fish.

Chapter 12: Aquaponics Technology And Design

Tanks with plants are placed above the tanks with fish. Seedlings are planted in the filler. Usually this is expanded clay. Water from the ultrasonic ultrasound system is pumped to the plants through a system of tubes and washes the roots, while nutrients are extracted from it. Expanded clay plays the role of a primitive biological filter, after passing through which, water returns to the pool with fish.

Another way, here, the role of a biological filter is played by sand. What is the essence of a bio-filter? In the process of decomposition, a large amount of toxic ammonia is released from the waste products of fish. Nitrifying bacteria multiply in the bio-filter (here in the sand), which sequentially decompose ammonia to nitrites and relatively harmless nitrates.

However, when the amount of nitrates exceeds the maximum permissible norm, they cease to be harmless. What to do? How to remove excess nitrates? The bio-filter does not perform such a function. And here plants come to the rescue. After all, nitrates are salts of nitric acid, and without nitrogen normal plant development is impossible, mutually beneficial process.

The benefits of combining aquaponics and ultrasound

Year-round plant growth

The water that comes to the roots from the pool is quite warm. The change of seasons does not play a role, because in the greenhouse, where the aquaponics installation is located, the necessary microclimate is artificially maintained. This makes it possible to get a tomato crop 4 times a year, and strawberries will bear fruit all the time. Imagine how much such a berry will cost in winter?

The possibility of obtaining increased yields

In aquaponics, yields are 60-70% higher than when growing the same plants in open ground and 40% higher than yields harvested in ordinary greenhouses.

Why is that?

Firstly, increased humidity.

Secondly - consistently high water temperature washing the roots.

Thirdly, naturally balanced organic substances dissolved in water.

Organic vegetables and fruits

UZV - a closed system. The content of pesticides, pesticides and salts of heavy metals in the water supplied to the plants is completely excluded. Due to this, the taste of berries and vegetables will be consistently high.

Market stability

Vegetables occupy an important share in the human diet. It is impossible to imagine a full meal without the participation of vegetables. And almost all of them can be grown using aquaponics.

Land saving

More exceeding land is being allocated for development, and fewer and fewer plots remain suitable for a garden or vegetable garden. Aquaponics successfully solves this problem - containers with plants can be placed over fish breeding pools in many tiers.

Water saving

Depending on the type of soil in your region and the amount of rainfall, up to 200 liters of water is spent per tomato plant during the growing season! And in the aquaponics system, the water "goes in a circle", which at times reduces its amount.

Lack of insect pests

The absence of soil warrants the absence of pests. So, you can be sure of the sincerity and safety of your crop.

What plants can be grown with aquaponics?

Almost any, if you decide to do this for commercial purposes, choose fast-growing and expensive species.

First of all, these are:

Leafy greens (all types of salad, dill, parsley, cilantro, etc.)

Tomatoes

Strawberries.

Good profit can be obtained when growing flowers for a cut. Cucumbers and cabbage, peppers and eggplant, onions and garlic - the field of activity is limitless.

It is not known what happens with root crops, there is no practical experience in their cultivation, but abroad they get good potato harvests.

Apparently, growing seedlings will not be very successful, since it will "hurt" when planting in the ground. The same thing happens with flowers for sale in pots.

Which fish species are preferred?

Of course – freshwater, it is unlikely that any of the plants will like salt water. Traditionally for ultrasound, they choose:

Trout

Sturgeons

Blackheads

Carp with carp for aquaponics is no worse

The choice is yours.

What is included in the aquaponic installation?

Tank for fish.

Culture of nitrifying bacteria - necessary for the decomposition of ammonia to nitrates assimilated by plants. You can buy it, or you can wait a couple of weeks, during which time the bacteria will multiply themselves in sufficient quantities.

Heater with temperature control - to maintain a constant temperature in the tank with fish.

Aerator or oxygen generator - for enriching water with oxygen. This is equally necessary for both fish and plants.

Equipment for regulating the pH level in water.

A pump for supplying water to plants.

Fish and feed for them.

The plants that you will grow.

What can you save on?

Quite an expensive component of the ultrasound are filters. Usually two types are used - mechanical and biological. When combining a UZV with an aquapone installation, the need for filters disappears, because their role will be played by the plants themselves.

Sample business plan

Let us calculate on the example of lettuce what profit can be obtained from a small aquaponics installation.

For normal functioning, for every cubic meter of water should be at least 1.7 m² of area planted with plants. In this space fit thousands of bushes of lettuce. In 35 days, the mass of each salad plant will reach 150 g. In total, this will be 150 kg. At supermarket prices - 67,500 rubles, and in a year it's quite possible to grow 10 crops. This is 675 thousand rubles of net profit.

Foreign experience

Aquaponics, as a business, is exotic for Russia so far. Some fish farmers grow mainly greens and strawberries for their own table.

But Europe and America attach increasing importance to quality control of products. Aquaponics-derived vegetables contain 10 times less nitrate than grown on open ground. Such "nitrate-free" vegetables cost them five times more than ordinary vegetables.

Aquaponics with long plywood trays

The first description of the installation for aquaponics was published in 1975. Water with fish waste was sent to trays with plants. The principle of the system was that the nutrients contained in the waste water play the role of fertilizer. Waste water was purified and released into the environment. Within a month, the plants showed signs of a lack of nutrients. This happened for several reasons. It turned out that in the 1970s, the nitrogen concentration in nitrogen fertilizers was 150 times lower than in modern preparations. Around the same time, Ph.D. John Todd and Nancy Jack Todd did a similar study at the New Alchemy Institute and developed a wastewater treatment system called the "living machine".

In 1978, a team of researchers led by Lewis focused on solving the problem of nitrogen deficiency. They worked with the first aquaponics system of dense stocking. Although the idea was correct, the nitrogen concentration remained low (6-10 mg / l), so additional fertilizer had to be used to maintain tomato growth. According to the generally accepted rule, the nitrate content in the system should be about 46 mg / l. The low nitrate content with dense stocking led to pronounced nitrogen starvation of plants, while a significant part of the nitrogen evaporated into the environment.

In 1986, Zweig developed a simple and effective aquaponics installation, determining, on the one hand, the ratio between the amount of fish feed and fish biomass, and on the other, the amount of nitrogen consumed by the vegetation. Iron deficiency was eliminated by replacing 20% of fish food with rabbit food. Although this step was an important milestone in the development of aquaponics technology, its role went unnoticed.

In 1985, scientists from the University of the Virgin Islands, led by Nair (let's call it the "UVO system"), developed a recirculating aquapone system. Like the Lewis system (1978), it had a rather complicated structure, and working with it required considerable investments: growing 1 kg of tilapia cost $ 3.18 (at 1985 prices). Despite the fact that the amount of nitrogen produced by the fish was ten times the amount needed for normal tomato growth, they still grew poorly. Unfortunately, at that time little was known about ways to prevent denitrification. Salts accumulated in the system, which impeded the growth of some plants (Jones 2005). The average iron content was 0.1 mg / L with a minimum acceptable level of 1-2 mg / L (Jones 2005). Scientists at North Carolina State University - Mark McMurtry, Douglas Nelson and Paul Nelson developed their own aquaponics system. They planted plants in gravel filler, which played the role of an internal bio-filter.

In 1993, Rakosi and Hargreaves, having studied the available scientific data on aquaponics, came to the conclusion that in order to develop criteria for constructing a system, it is necessary to analyze the volumes of nutrients consumed by plants and to track their circulation in the system. A group of researchers led by Rakosi (1993) tried to track the movement of nutrients in systems created at the University of the Virgin Islands (conventionally called SVR) and compare the indicators obtained with good or poor plant growth. Unfortunately, all systems yielded different results, and it was not possible to identify any general trends.

Subsequently, a study was conducted to determine the optimal ratio between the number of fish and the area occupied by plants. Today it can be assumed that the amount of nutrients produced by fish exceeded the indices necessary for normal plant growth in all experiments. All grown lettuce heads had the same weight, regardless of the number of fish in the system. Vegetables grown in aquaponics were smaller than vegetables grown in hydroponics (172-248 g, Kratky 2005), indicating a lack of nutrients. After improvement, it was possible to grow heads of slightly larger mass (181-344 g, Rakocy et. Al. 1997). After a few years, the SVR system has proven its effectiveness and durability (Rakocy et. Al. 2004). By then, it consisted of four pools with fish, six trays for plants, a treatment tank, containers with filter screens, a tank for cleaning water from gases, a sewage tank, a tank with soil, a water pump, two compressors and more than 200 aerators. Such a system could be managed only by qualified specialists. Rakosi was the first who managed to develop a multifunctional system, so he is called the "godfather" of aquaponics.

Vegetables were generally grown in water on floating plastic pallets (Rakocy 1989). Water was carefully aerated so that the roots of the plants were fed with oxygen; in addition, it was necessary to maintain the necessary nitrogen balance. Kratky (2005) practiced a system in which plant roots were not immersed in water, but doused with moisture-saturated air. This method was called the "nutrient film." Lennard and Leonard (2006) tested three types of systems, some of which were later used. The following methods were tested: pouring gravel soil with water, the "feeding film" technique, in which the roots were not immersed in water, but doused with moist air, and only the tips of the roots slightly touched the surface of the water; as well as systems with floating pallets. Systems that used water-filled gravel proved to be the most effective. Ako tested the following methods: drip and gravel irrigation, the ebb-tide system, which allowed pouring and exposing the surface of the gravel layer, growing plants on floating pallets with holes, as well as ordinary pallets. He rated the first two methods as the best, while the first, in his opinion, turned out to be the least expensive.

Since Rakosi improved this technology, more than 20 years have passed, but at the moment there is not a single example of the successful use of aquaponic systems based on his method. This article was written and published in order to rectify this situation. However, in fairness it should be noted that from an economic point of view, aquaponics is quite difficult to implement, since due to low prices for vegetables, relatively low returns, high investment and operating costs, it is not very profitable to deal with it (Tokunaga et. Al.). Since vegetables grown in some regions of Oceania are transported mainly by air, they have a very high cost. The advantage of aquaponics is that it gives products that are unique in taste, since they are grown exclusively on organic materials without the use of pesticides. Based on the foregoing, the task of researchers is to present a system that would not require large capital investments, and whose work and management would be based on purely biological and chemical factors. The work of aquaponics should be determined by a stable cycle of chemicals, and in case of a chemical imbalance at hand, you must constantly have the means to prevent it.

Design

Modern aquaponics systems are modeled on the very cheap Kratky systems (2005). He used simple wooden crates. Shallow wooden crates act as trays for vegetables , the bottom of which is made of plywood (1.9 cm thick, 121.92 cm long and 243.84 cm wide), mounted on two side planks (5.8 × 10.16x253.84 cm), as well as the front and rear planks (5.8 × 10.16x121.92 cm). Such a tray can be made very quickly and without significant financial costs (about $ 84). In each tray, 48 heads of lettuce can be grown. Some vegetables, such as Chinese cabbage (Pak Choy or Brassica juncea), after 5 weeks weigh more than 2 kg.

Mark the locations of the screw holes around the bottom perimeter at a distance of about 41 cm from each other. Use stainless steel screws 5.1 cm / 0.44 cm or 5.1 cm / 0.52 cm. In the photo below the bottom of the tray for vegetables and the walls are ready for screed. It is recommended to collect the boxes in an upside down position.

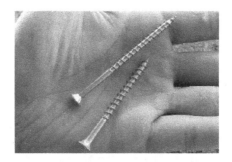

Cover the bottom and inner walls of the box with plastic film and fix it as seen below

Typically, the trays are attached to each other so that their bottoms are on the same level. Interconnected vegetable trays, as a rule, the channel consists of 8 trays, based on the fact that the standard length of the roll of plastic film is 30.48 m. It is vital that the bottom of the trays occupy a stringently horizontal position, otherwise the water from the fish will drain into puddles. Trays are mounted on silicate blocks with two holes.

The photo shows the first aquaponics farm that uses the Ako and Baker system (2009). The trays have been in operation for about 5 years and are still in excellent condition, since the design eliminates the contact of the boxes with water. Tray Covers Plants are placed in small mesh pots mounted on foam pallets, as shown in below. The trays are filled with water until the surface of the water touches the bottom of the mesh pots, so that the roots are in the water and can receive nutrients. A gap of about 5 cm wide remains between the pallet and the surface of the water, which contributes to good ventilation of the soil.

Recently, researchers found that growing plants on volcanic ash, which is under a layer of water 1.5 cm thick, gives a stable and very good crop. This design was called a drip-gravel irrigation system (drip filters are used). The ebb-tide system, in which bell siphons are involved, is also effective, but the authors of the work preferred to use drip systems, since they create good conditions for worms that process fish waste, as seen below shows the ebb-tide system.

Water is pumped from the pool with fish and feeds the plants, after which, through a special riser with a jumper, it returns to the tank with fish. In the process of developing the project, the idea came up of installing pallets for seedlings. They look like foam pallets, only have much more holes and contain 98 small shoots (as long as the size of the plants allows). Seedling pallets are placed on the walls of the trays, and in order to prevent the pallets from sagging, three 10-cm plastic flower pots can be placed in each tray. Most aquaponists use seedling boxes, consisting of several isolated cells filled with soil. Soil serves as a source of organic material in the system. For about three weeks, in boxes for seedlings it is necessary to maintain high humidity, after which the culture can be planted in large trays. Most plants produce a crop that can be sold three weeks after planting in trays. A significant part of farmers prefers to automate the planting of seeds, since manual placement of seeds into the cells is a very tedious and long process. Aquaponics is an extremely time-consuming activity, so automation is indispensable here. When growing salads in tropical regions, such as Hawaii or the islands of Oceania, it is necessary to provide partial shading (Wolff and Coltman 1990). During studies at the University of Hawaii, Manoa lettuce showed growth at 50% shading. In the fifth image above shows shaded systems. Initially, the aquapone method was used to grow red leaf lettuce. It turned out that he is well taking root. The same can be said about other types of lettuce, for example Manoa or loosened "romaine", pak choy and bok choy (Brassica juncea) cabbage, as well as basil. In addition to salads, other farmers grow beets, cucumbers, tomatoes, lingonberries, strawberries and watercress. The most frequent difficulties faced by professionals using systems with floating pallets is mosquitoes, as water often stagnates in trays. The mosquito population can be controlled by holding three male guppies in each tray, as they feed on mosquito larvae. Different-sex individuals should not be kept in trays, as they begin to multiply and eat plant roots.

Optimal system ratios

The authors recommend a nutrient circulation scheme that balances the amount of feed consumed (Silver Cup pellets in the amount of 42 grams per day with 42% protein content) and the amount of metabolites entering the system. These metabolites must be restored and cleaned with the help of a gravel bed or a 16-liter deep bio-filter with a capacity of 321 l with fish (image below). The filter is a mesh cylinder measuring 25x32cm, made of extruded plastic and filled with PVC fragments. For aeration, you can use a pump with a power of 25 watts and three air sprayers (15.24 cm). The volume of water in the tank should be about 200 liters. The initial landing density is 2.5 kg. To prevent the growth of microalgae, it is recommended to shade the containers with fish.

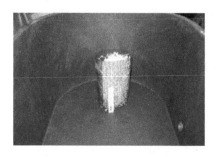

It is necessary to start feeding with small portions, gradually increasing the quantity, so that after two weeks the daily portion is 6.5 tablespoons (42 g) of food daily. This is only an approximate amount, since the fish itself determines the amount of food acceptable for themselves. A gradual increase in portions promotes the multiplication of bacteria that are introduced into the system from the environment and are involved in the process of purifying water from harmful impurities.

Feeding should be conducted out twice a day: in the morning, when the water is just starting to warm up, and in the evening. It is best to determine the required amount of food by placing the recommended portion in the container, then wait 10 minutes and calculate the amount of remaining food. If after 10 minutes 5-10% of the feed remains from the serving, you can save the current dose. If more than 10% of the feed remains from the initial dose, the serving should be reduced. If the residue is less than 5%, increase the serving. Every week you need to add fertilizer - chelated iron to the trays.

Twice a week, water quality must be checked. This procedure allows you to track the content of toxic substances, such as ammonia and nitrites, and to ensure that their level decreases as the microflora of the biofilter grows. The authors use an oxygen meter YSI 55. Despite the high cost, this device is necessary for aquaponics. For proper nutrition of the fish, it is necessary to maintain the level of dissolved oxygen in the pool with it not lower than 5 mg / l and not lower than 2 mg / l in other containers in order to prevent denitrification. Researchers Use Portable pH Metersto measure the concentration of hydrogen ions (Pinpoint, American Marine Inc, Ridgefield, CT, USA) and try to maintain a level of at least 6.0. If the pH drops below an acceptable level, to restore the optimum level, potassium carbonate is added to the water in the ratio of 1 teaspoon to 80 teaspoons of feed. A decrease in pH leads to a deterioration or loss of appetite in fish. Ammonia and nitrite levels can be measured using inexpensive Tetra or API systems, although Hach and LaMotte are more accurate and meet gold quality standards. The conversion of total ammonia to deionized ammonia is expressed using the Henderson-Hasselbach equation:

pH = pKa + log (deionized ammonia / total ammonia)

The pH level is measured by the device, while the pKa level for ammonia is 9.25. The level of total ammonia (or total ammonia nitrogen) is measured using instruments. After calculating the level of non-ionized ammonia, it should be noted that a concentration of 1.46 mg / L is lethal for tilapia (Evans et. Al. 2006). To calculate the nitrite nitrogen level, you need to multiply the current nitrite level indicator by 0.31. A concentration of nitrite nitrogen of 16 mg / L is fatal for tilapia (Lewis et. Al, 1986). It can be measured using Salifert instruments, although Lamotte instruments are more accurate, but less reliable. A value of 47 mg / l is optimal, but flushing the system leads to a decrease. The authors of the work successfully tested the system for aquaponics at a concentration of nitrate nitrogen of 15 mg / L. The population of regenerating microflora and the optimal concentration of nutrients stabilize after about a month. Toxins should be kept to a minimum.

1. Are the plants in the sun? Plants require lighting of 30,000 lux. The authors used a photometer.

2. Is the pool with fish darkened? If the pool is not darkened, algae will start to grow

3. Does the fish feed until it is saturated? Checking the feed intake in 10 minutes will determine the saturation of the fish. If the feed is low, the nitrate level for the plants will be low.

4. What is the level of nitrate? If the concentration is low <15 mg / L, slight denitrification will be observed. In these conditions, the authors use a DO meter to determine the points of decrease in the concentration of dissolved oxygen.

5. Drip-gravel irrigation is most effective.

Keeping fish also requires special knowledge and skills to create a balanced ecosystem. Which fish is best to use?

Tilapia is the second most popular fish grown in the world. Tilapia is ideal for aquaponic systems. It is easy to breed; it grows well, does not always withstand the favorable conditions of the aquatic environment, is omnivorous and actively eats food.

Koi is one of the species of carp that lives in Asian countries and is found in large decorative reservoirs. For those who like this fish, the aquapone system is a good way to grow it.

Trout-also used for breeding in aquatic systems with cool water temperatures. Trout needs a temperature from 10 ° C to 20 ° C. It gains weight very quickly and is unpretentious to feed, which quickly processes it.

Other species suitable for such systems are mussels, freshwater shrimp and crayfish.

Do not forget that the quality of the feed is important not only for the health of fish, but also for the health of farmed plants.

The composition of the feed includes proteins, fats, minerals, etc., which consume fish in the wild in a natural way. Sources of such nutrition in aquaponic systems can serve as fishmeal, corn, soy and other substances of animal origin after their processing.

All fish feeds, especially brands that use more natural ingredients and less preservatives, have a specific, limited shelf life. They require being stored in a cool, dry room.

There are many tips and recipes for feeding fish. The most effective recipe: it is better to use as much food as fish eat in 5 minutes. Residues of feed must be removed from the tank in which the fish lives.

How to increase acidity (pH) in an aqueous medium?

To increase the pH, use calcium carbonate and potassium carbonate, alternate them or add in equal amounts at the same time.

They are used more often for a number of reasons:

They give strength to the buffer system.

They are not toxic and do not leave burns or ulcers on the surface of the skin, unlike hydroxides.

They are included in the list of the Institute for the Review of Organic Additives as suitable additives for growing organics.

How to reduce the pH in aquaponics?

In addition to aquarium options - peat and CO_2, it is advised to use acids: nitric, hydrochloric or phosphoric. Aqua rovers use phosphoric, because it is the safest of these acids and it brings a small amount of phosphates into the systems, which are not indifferent to plants. But phosphates contribute to the growth of algae. So if you actively grow algae in the system, it is better to use a different acid.

In the window of our store there are solutions for aquaponics to change and control the acidity of the environment.

You do not need to use citric acid, because it causes the death of bacteria. No need to use vinegar, because it is weak as an acid. The fish will pickle faster than lower the pH level.

Changes in pH negatively affect the condition of the underwater inhabitants, so be careful about this indicator, change the indicator for a certain period: add a small amount to the system, wait until the substance is evenly distributed throughout the aquarium, then measure the pH level. Repeat until you get the desired result.

The amount of reagent used to change the acidity of the aqueous medium will vary depending on the stage of growth processes and the level of carbon dioxide in the water.

What pH is desirable in aquaponics?

Managing aquaponics technology is not easy, as you need to monitor the three main groups of living things: plants, fish and bacteria. While plants "love" the slightly acidic reaction of the medium (from 5.5 to 6.5), fish and bacteria are positive about the slightly alkaline environment (7.0-8.0). It is important to find the average between the three living organisms. It is best to keep the pH at 6.8 - 7.0. Such an indicator will make it possible for all inhabitants of the system to live in normal conditions.

How many times and with what substances to feed fish in aquaponics?

It all depends on what type of food fish prefer. Carnivores (trout, perch and bass) need food with a high concentration of protein (45 - 50%). Omnivorous fish (tilapia, perch, carp, and catfish) absorb less protein feed (usually 32% protein). Keep in mind that protein is important for young, growing fish.

Feeding should be minimal during the first months. It is necessary to feed the fish so that they ate all the food in 5 minutes. This is not more than 1 tbsp. tablespoons of 20 fish per day. Keep in mind that fish can live for several weeks without eating.

Water may turn green for a while, but this is not a constant occurrence. As soon as the water in the system is clear, the number of feeds can be increased up to 2-3 times a day. But keep an eye on how much fish eat the feed in 5 minutes. As a rule, adult tilapia eats about 1% of their body weight per day, and fry are able to eat up to 7% of body weight.

How to start a growing cycle in such a system?

After you have all the necessary devices to start the process in a cyclic mode, you need to enter the source of ammonia. Usually, fish are placed in containers for this, which will add the necessary element to the aquatic environment.

Is aeration important?

So that fish, plants and bacteria do not get sick and grow quickly on aquaponics, they need a certain level of oxygen dissolved in water. Both in fish containers and in the water at the base of plant roots, the oxygen level should be at the level of 5 mg / l or higher.

A suitable oxygen level is also important for maintaining the life of beneficial nitrifying bacteria that convert toxic ammonia and nitrite to nitrate ions. Ammonia, isolated through gills by fish, transforms one genus of bacteria (Nitrosomonas) into nitrites, and another bacterial species (Nitrobacter) converts nitrites to nitrates. All of these chemical reactions require oxygen.

Need biological control?

To control diseases of fish and plants in aquaponics, the use of pesticides is prohibited, since many of them are toxic. Also, you cannot use most of the chemicals to treat fish (if necessary) for parasites and diseases, because these agents can destroy beneficial bacteria. In addition, plants are able to absorb and accumulate them.

Biological control methods are the only possible option for controlling pests and diseases. Biological control so far is a subject for serious research. New methods are created and tested, experimental work is underway. As an example, this is the breeding of hardy fish that are resistant to many negative factors.

The top fish to breed in aquaponics

The tilapia is probably the most common fish in aquaponics. It can measure up to 50 centimeters long. Tilapia is a freshwater or brackish water fish, but of the hundreds of species of tilapia, only a small number are compatible in aquaponics. In fact, tilapia is a kind of exotic carp that grows very quickly. In fact, tilapia loves hot water.

Trout is also very common in aquaponics. His chair is appreciated all over the world and its growth is also rapid. You can go from a trout to a trout of respectable size (it is then called portion trout) to be consumed in less than a year. In general, in aquaponics, we often see the rainbow species from fish farming is a hybrid trout species obtained from crossing and which does not reproduce naturally. For it to reproduce, it must be in its natural environment, in North America for example, otherwise it must be done in the laboratory with test tubes and insemination accessories ... Hang on, the rainbow trout en-ciel can exceed 120 cm and 25 kg and has a life expectancy of more than ten years.

The sun, silver or golden pole. The poles are beautiful and are starting to take up more and more space in the world of aquaponics. The aquaponists appreciate them very much and many are those to launch out in the breeding of poles. Perches are caught in both fresh and brackish waters. There are an impressive number of perch derivatives around the world.

Common carp and love carp or even Koi carp. The carp groups together under its name several species. She lives about twenty years but some are over 70 years old. Some even say they have already seen centuries-old carp. It is appreciated in fish farming because it does not have its characteristic vase taste when it is raised in a clean basin, without vase. An urban legend says that Koi carp is not edible... the debate is open. Who wants to test?

The black bass is a very lively and combative fish. In Europe it never exceeds 30 to 50 centimeters and can weigh between 500 grams and 3 kilos. They are rarely seen in aquaponics but they can be bred in aquaponics.

Bream. These fish being bioaccumulators, they are often prohibited for consumption because in their polluted natural habitats, they take up heavy metals and then become unfit for consumption. Fortunately in aquaponics, they can be raised and are much appreciated.

Mole is a rather rare fish in Europe because the consumption of its pulpit is prohibited there. It is however very famous in Japan or in Taiwan where it is said that its pulpit is seen as a delicacy. The largest known mole weighs 400 kilos and measures more than 1.80 meters.

Catfish or catfish are often frowned upon in Europe by fishermen but they are well suited for rearing in ponds provided that they are not raised until adulthood where they can easily exceed 1.5 meters long.

Barramundi can be up to 2 meters long and weigh up to 60 kilos, but its average weight is 5 to 6 kilos. It can be raised in aquaponics without worries.

Pacu is a species of fish related to piranha but they are often omnivorous or herbivorous. There are quite a few strange stories around the pacus in the world... I'll let you find out

Yellow perch is often thought of as a small perch. It reproduces very easily and can fill your aquaponic tanks.

Various ornamental fish such as angelfish, guppies, grouse, sturgeon, molly, etc.

Also note that you can do astaciculture in aquaponics, that is to say crayfish farming.

Nitrates and nitrites in aquaponics

Nitrates and nitrites are the basis of our aquaponics ecosystems. We will see below everything you need to know about nitrates and nitrites in order to avoid possible toxicity for the fish in the system and for the end consumer: humans.

Nitrates (NO3) are the essential end product of the nitrogen cycle but, unlike ammonia and nitrites, they do not really begin to be toxic until relatively high concentrations and over the longer term. Fish are more resistant to high levels of nitrates than to high levels of nitrites, it's not the same. Like temperature or pH issues, the resistance of fish to an overload of nitrates is specific to the species of farmed fish.

If you want to know more:

In the singular, nitrate denotes the ion and the nitrate radical and in the plural, nitrates denote the salts and esters containing nitrate ions (sodium nitrate, potassium nitrate, etc.) or the nitrate radical (ethyl nitrate, nitrate amyl, cellulose nitrate, etc.). These are the salts and esters of nitric acid. The old names for nitrates are niter or saltpeter. The chemical formula for nitrate ion is NO3?

The presence of an excess of nitrates in the water is an indication of pollution of agricultural (fertilizer), urban (dysfunction of the sanitation networks) or industrial origin. In Europe, the Nitrates directive aims to reduce this pollution.

What is the right level of nitrates?

In many countries, water intended for human consumption must respect limit values (for example 50 mg / L in France and in Europe) to be qualified as potable. The WHO also recommends not exceeding this threshold of 50 mg / L.

In aquaponics, it is said that a level of nitrates above 150 ppm is high. The level of perfect nitrates is between 40 and 120 ppm. You should never exceed 800. Some aquaponists are at 20 ppm and the plants grow very well but you should know that in hydroponics, some cultivators greatly exceed 600 ppm to cultivate at 800 ppm without harming the plants or the fish. Of course, in aquaponics, you have to find the right compromise between the right level of nitrates for plants and the right level of nitrates for fish, that's why we should always have a level of nitrates between 40 and 120 ppm in aquaponics.

For information, the maximum level of nitrates for a trout is 800 ppm and 1000 ppm for plants.

What Are Nitrites?

Nitrites (NO2?) Are salts of nitrous acid that result from the reduction of ammonia by nitrobacteria. These same nitrites will then be transformed into nitrates by these same nitrobacteria.

Too much nitrite in the water and its guaranteed asphyxiation for your fish. Note that in humans and mammals, the presence of nitrites in the blood prevents hemoglobin from properly fixing oxygen.

The maximum level of nitrites for your system is 1 ppm for fish, 5 ppm for plants, and 10 ppm for nitrifying bacteria and 1 ppm for mineralizing bacteria. In your system you should aim for an ideal rate of less than 0.25 ppm.

Reduce the nitrate level in your aquaponics water

If you have too many nitrates in your pool, you can start by removing water to replace it with fresh, be careful not to replace too much water at once because the balance of your system would be threatened. Then measure the pH and the hardness of the water as well as the level of nitrates in order to find a balance.

Then, the second solution is to decrease the food you give your fish, in fact, by feeding them less, you will reduce the volume of fish droppings so the nitrate level will drop and the system will stabilize.

You can also lower the level of nitrates by using plants that are rich in nitrates such as floating plants, tomatoes, peppers or even corn... etc. The list is long but is aware that the level of nitrates will not suddenly drop, there is no miracle, it will be necessary to allow the plants time to assimilate these nitrates.

However, if these solutions are not satisfactory, we advise you to use filters aimed at decreasing the amount of nitrates that you can find in specialized aquarium stores. These filters are not necessary in my opinion but you can always use them as the case may be.

In summary, here are the tips to lower the level of nitrates in your water:

By changing a large volume of water (1/3 or even 1/2 of the volume of the basin)

By feeding your fish less for a week or two

By adding more plants to your growing container

By buying a nitrates filter

Conclusion

Thank you again for purchasing this book on aquaponics.

I am extremely excited to pass this information along to you, and I am so happy that you now have read and can hopefully implement these strategies going forward.

I hope this book was able to help you understand aquaponics and how to set one up inn you home.

The next step is to get started using this information and to hopefully live a exciting life!

Please don't be someone who just reads this information and doesn't apply it, the strategies in this book will only benefit you if you use them!

If you know of anyone else that could benefit from the information presented here please inform them of this book.

Thank you and good luck!

CPSIA information can be obtained
at www.ICGtesting.com
Printed in the USA
LVHW051913090522
718310LV00011B/1392